by Rev. Andrew Murray

"BE
PERFECT
AS YOUR
HEAVENLY
FATHER IS
PERFECT"

A
DEVOTIONAL
STUDY OF
CHRIST'S
COMMAND

FAITH CHRISTIAN BOOKS
3022 - 176th ST., SURREY, B.C.
PHONE 576-6063
DIMENSION BOOKS
Bethany Fellowship, Inc.
Minneapolis, Minnesota

DIMENSION BOOKS
are published by
Bethany Fellowship, Inc.
6820 Auto Club Road
Minneapolis, Minn. 55438

Printed in the
United States of America

Preface

If anyone takes up this little volume with
the idea of finding a theory of perfection expounded or vindicated, he will be disappointed.
My object has been a very different one. What
I have wished to do is to go with my reader
through the Word of God, noting the principal
passages in which the word "perfect" occurs,
and seeking in each case from the context to
find what the impression is the word was meant
to convey. It is only when we have yielded ourselves simply and prayerfully to allow the words
of Scripture to have their full force that we
are on the right track for combining the different aspects of truth into one harmonious
whole.

Among the thoughts which have specially
been brought home to me in these meditations,
and in which I trust I may secure the assent of
my reader, the following are the chief.

1. *There is a perfection of which Scripture
speaks as possible and attainable.* There may
be, there is, great diversity of opinion as to
how the term is to be defined. But there can

be only one opinion as to the fact that God asks and expects His children to be perfect with Him; that He promises it as His own work; and that Scripture speaks of some as having been perfect before Him, and having served Him with a perfect heart. Scripture speaks of a perfection that is at once our duty and our hope.

2. *To know what this perfection is we must begin by accepting the command and obeying it with our whole heart.* Our natural tendency is the very opposite. We want to discuss and define what perfection is, to understand how the command can be reconciled with our assured conviction that no man is perfect, to provide for all the dangers we are sure to be found in the path of perfection.

This is not God's way. Jesus said, "If any man will *do,* ... he shall *know.*" The same principle holds good in all human attainment. It is only he who has accepted in adoring submission and obedience the command *"Be perfect,"* who can hope to know what the perfection is that God asks and gives. Until the Church is seen prostrate before God, seeking this blessing as her highest good, it will be no wonder if the very word perfection, instead of being an attraction and a joy, is a cause of apprehension and anxiety, of division and offense. God increase the number of those who, in childlike humility, take the word from His own lips, as a living seed, in the assurance that it will bring forth much fruit.

3. *Perfection is no arbitrary demand; in the very nature of things God can ask nothing less.* And this is true, whether we think of Him or of ourselves.

If we think of Him, who as God has created the universe for himself and His glory, who seeks and alone is able to fill it with His happiness and love, we see how impossible it is for God to allow aught else to share man's heart with himself. God must be all and have all. As Lawgiver and Judge, He dare not be content with aught less than absolute legal perfection. As Redeemer and Father it equally becomes Him to claim nothing less than a real childlike perfection. God must have all.

If we think of ourselves, the call to perfection is no less imperative. God is such an infinite, spiritual good, and the soul is so incapable of receiving or knowing or enjoying Him except as it gives itself wholly to Him, that for our own sakes God's love can demand of us nothing less than a perfect heart.

4. *Perfection, as the highest aim of what God in His great power would do for us, is something so divine, spiritual, and heavenly, that it is only the soul that yields itself very tenderly to the leading of the Holy Spirit that can hope to know its blessedness.*

God hath wrought into every human heart a deep desire after perfection. That desire is manifested in the admiration which all men have for excellence in the different objects or pursuits to which they attach value. In the believer who yields himself wholly to God this desire fastens itself upon God's wonderful promises, and inspires a prayer like that of McCheyne: "Lord, make me as holy as a pardoned sinner can be made." The more we learn to long for this full conformity to God's will, for the consciousness that we are always pleasing to Him, we shall see that all this must come as a gift direct from heaven, as the full outbirth in us of the life of God, the inbreathing of the Holy Spirit of Jesus in those who are wholly yielded to His indwelling and rule. Trusting ever less to men's thoughts and teachings, we shall retire much into the secret of God's presence, in the assurance that the more we see God's face and hear the secret voice that comes direct from Him, *"be perfect,"* the more will the Holy Spirit dwelling within us unfold the heavenly fullness and power of the words, and make them, as God's words, bring and give and work the very thing He speaks.

In the hope that these simple meditations may help some of God's children to go on to perfection, I commit them and myself to the blessed Father's teaching and keeping.

ANDREW MURRAY

Wellington, 1893

Contents

Contents

Philippians

Colossians

Hebrews

James

Peter

John

A Prayer

EVER BLESSED FATHER! Thou hast sent me a message by Thy beloved Son that I am to be perfect as Thou art. Coming from Thee, O Thou incomprehensible and most glorious God, it means more than man can grasp. Coming to Thee, I ask that Thou wouldst thyself teach me what it means, work in me what it claims, give me what it promises.

My Father! I accept the word in the obedience of faith. I would yield my life to its rule. I would hide it in my heart as a living seed, in the assurance that there, deeper than thought or feeling, Thy Holy Spirit can make it strike root and grow up.

And as I go through Thy Word, to meditate on what it says of the path of the perfect, teach me, O my Father, to bring every thought of mine captive to the obedience of Christ, and to wait for that teaching of Thy Holy Spirit which is so sure to the upright in heart. In Him, with whom Thou hast sent me the message, give me the answer to this prayer too. Amen.

CHAPTER ONE

BE PERFECT!

A Perfect Heart Makes a
Perfect Man

"Noah was a righteous man, and perfect in his generation, and Noah walked with God" (Gen. 6:9).

"And the Lord said unto Satan, Hast thou considered my servant Job, that there is none like him in the earth, a perfect and an upright man, one that feareth God and escheweth evil?" (Job 1:8).

"The heart of David was perfect with the Lord his God" (I Kings 11:4; 15:3).

"Asa's heart was perfect with the Lord all his days" (I Kings 15:14).

WE HAVE GROUPED TOGETHER four men, all of whom Holy Scripture testifies that they were perfect men or that their heart was perfect with God. Of each of them Scripture testifies, too, that they were not perfect in the

sense of absolute sinlessness. We know how
Noah fell. We know how Job had to humble himself before God. We know how sadly David
sinned. And of Asa we read that there came
a time when he did foolishly and relied on
the Syrians and not on the Lord his God;
when in his disease he sought not to the Lord
but to the physicians. And yet the heart of
these men was perfect with the Lord their God.[1]

To understand this, there is one thing we
must remember. The meaning of the word perfect must in each case be decided by that partic-
ular stage in God's education of His people in
which it is used. What a father or a teacher
counts perfection in a child of ten is very different from what he would call so in one of twenty.
As to the disposition or spirit, the perfection
would be the same; in its contents, as the proofs
by which it was to be judged of, there would
be a wide difference. We shall see later on how
in the Old Testament nothing was really made
perfect; how Christ has come to reveal, and work
out, and impart the true perfection; how the
perfection, as revealed in the New Testament,
is something infinitely higher, more spiritual
and efficacious, than under the old economy.
And yet at root they are one. God looketh at
the heart. A heart that is perfect with Him is
an object of complacency and approval. A wholehearted consecration to His will and fellowship,

a life that takes as its motto, "Wholly for God," has in all ages, even where the Spirit had not yet been given to dwell in the heart, been accepted by Him as the mark of the perfect man.

The lesson which these Scripture testimonies suggest to us is a very simple but a very searching one. In God's record of the lives of His servants there are some of whom it is written: "His heart was perfect with the Lord his God." In this, let each reader ask, what does God see and say of me? Does my life, in the sight of God, bear the mark of intense, wholehearted consecration to God's will and service? of a burning desire to be as perfect as it is possible for grace to make me? Let us yield ourselves to the searching light of this question. Let us believe that with this word *perfect* God means something very real and true. Let us not evade its force, or hide ourselves from its condemning power, by the vain subterfuge that we do not fully know what it means. *We must first accept it, and give up our lives to it,* before we can understand it. It cannot be insisted upon too strongly that, whether in the Church at large and its teaching, or in the life of the individual believer, there can be no hope of comprehending what perfection is except as we count all things loss to be apprehended of it, to live for it, to accept of it, to possess it.

But so much we can understand. What I do with a perfect heart I do with love and delight, with a willing mind and all my strength. It implies a fixedness of purpose and a concentration of effort that makes everything subordinate to the one object of my choice. This is what God asks, what His saints have given, what we must give.

Again I say to everyone who wishes to join me in following through the Word of God its revelation of His will concerning perfection, "Yield yourself to the searching question: Can God say of me as of Noah and Job, of David and Asa, that my heart is perfect with the Lord my God? Have I given myself up to say that there must be nothing, nothing whatever, to share my heart with God and His will? Is a heart perfect with the Lord my God the object of my desire, my prayer, my faith, my hope?" Whether it has been so or not, let it be so today. Make the promise of God's Word your own: "The God of peace himself perfect you." The God, who is of power to do above all we ask or think, will open up to you the blessed prospect of a life of which He shall say: "His heart was perfect with the Lord his God."

CHAPTER TWO

BE PERFECT!

Walk Before Me, and Be Thou Perfect

"And when Abram was ninety years old and nine, the Lord appeared unto Abram, and said unto him, I am Almighty God: walk before me, and be thou perfect. And I will make my covenant between me and thee, and will multiply thee exceedingly. And Abram fell on his face: and God talked with him" (Gen. 17: 1–3).

"Thou shalt be perfect with the Lord thy God" (Deut. 18: 13).

"Let your heart be perfect with the Lord our God to walk in his statutes" (I Kings 8: 61).

IT WAS NOW TWENTY-FOUR YEARS since God had called Abram to go out from his father's home, and that he had obeyed. All that time he had been a learner in the school of faith. The time was approaching for him to inherit the promise, and God comes to establish His covenant with him. In view of this, God meets him with this threefold word: I am Almighty God: walk before me: ... be thou perfect.

Be thou perfect. The connection in which we find the word will help us to understand its meaning. God reveals himself as God Almighty. Abram's faith had long been tried: it was about to achieve one of its greatest triumphs—faith was to be changed to vision in the birth of Isaac. God invites Abram more than ever to remember, and to rest upon, His omnipotence. He is Almighty God; all things are possible to Him; He holds rule over all. All His power is working for those who trust Him. And all He asks of His servant is that he shall be perfect with Him, give Him his whole heart, his perfect confidence.

God Almighty with all His power is wholly for thee; be thou wholly for God. The knowledge and faith of what God is lies at the root of what we are to be: *"I am Almighty God: be thou perfect."* As I know Him whose power fills heaven and earth, I see that this is the one thing needed: to be perfect with Him, wholly and entirely given up to Him. *Wholly for God* is the keynote of perfection.

Walk before me, and be thou perfect. It is in the life fellowship with God, in His realized presence and favor, that it becomes possible to be perfect with Him. Walk before me: Abraham had been doing this. God's word calls him to a clearer and more conscious apprehension of this as his life calling. It is easy for us to study what Scripture says of perfection, to form our ideas of it, and argue for them. But let us remember that it is only as we are walking closely with God, seeking and in some measure attaining, uninterrupted communion with Him, that the divine command will come to us in its divine power, and unfold to us its divine meaning. Walk before Me, *and* be thou perfect. God's realized presence is the school, is the secret, of perfection. It is only he who studies what perfection is *in the full light of God's presence* to whom its hidden glory will be opened up.

That realized presence is the great blessing of the redemption in Jesus Christ. The veil has been rent, the way into the true sanctuary, the presence of God, has been opened; we have access with boldness into the Holiest of all. God who has proved himself God Almighty in raising Jesus from the dead and setting Him, and us in Him, at His right hand, speaks now to us: "I am God Almighty: *walk before me, and be thou perfect.*"

That command came not only to Abraham. Moses gave it to the whole people of Israel: "Thou shalt be perfect with the Lord thy God." It is for all Abraham's children; for all the Israel

of God; *for every believer.* Oh! think not that
ere you can obey you must first understand and
define what perfection means. No, God's way
is the very opposite of this. Abraham went out,
not knowing whither he went. Thou art called
to go on to perfection: go out, not knowing
whither thou goest. It is a land God will show
thee.

Let thy heart be filled with His glory: I
am God Almighty. Let thy life be spent in His
presence: walk before Me. As His power and
His presence rest upon thee and fill thee, thy
heart will, ere thou knowest, be drawn up, and
strengthened to accept and rejoice in and fulfill
the command: be thou perfect. As surely as the
opening bud has but to abide in the light of the
sun to attain perfection, will the soul that walks
in the light of God be perfect too. As the God,
who is all, shines upon it, it cannot but rejoice
to give Him all.

CHAPTER THREE

BE PERFECT!

Perfect with the Lord Thy God

"Thou shalt be perfect with the Lord thy God" (Deut. 18:13).

T O BE PERFECT BEFORE GOD is not only the calling and the privilege of a man like Abraham, it is equally the duty of all his children. The command is given to all Israel, for each man of God's people to receive and obey: "Thou shalt be perfect with the Lord thy God." It comes to each child of God; no one professing to be a Christian may turn aside from it, or refuse it obedience, without endangering his salvation. It is not a command like, "Thou shalt not kill," or, "Thou shalt not steal," having reference to a limited sphere in our life, but is a principle that lies at the very root of all true religion. If our service of God is to be acceptable, it must not be with a divided, but a whole, a perfect heart.

25

The chief hindrance in the way of obedience to this command lies in our misapprehension of what religion is. Man was created simply to live for God, to show forth His glory, by allowing God to show how completely He could reveal His likeness and blessedness in man. God lives for man; longing in the greatness of His love to communicate His goodness and His love.

It was to this life, lost by sin, Christ came to redeem us back. The selfishness of the human heart looks upon salvation as simply the escape from hell, with so much of holiness as is needful to make our happiness secure. Christ meant us to be restored to the state from which we had fallen—the whole heart, the whole will, the whole life given up to the glory and service of God. To be wholly given up to God, to be perfect with the Lord our God, lies at the very root, is the very essence of true religion. The enthusiastic devotion of the whole heart to God is what is asked of us.

When once this misconception has been removed, and the truth begins to dawn upon the soul, a second hindrance is generally met with in the question of unbelief: How can these things be? Instead of first accepting God's command and then waiting in the path of obedience for the teaching of the Spirit, men are at once ready with their own interpretation of the Word, and confidently affirm: It cannot be. They forget that the whole object of the gospel and the glory of Christ's redemption is that it makes possible what is beyond man's thoughts or powers; and that it reveals God, not as a Lawgiver and Judge, exacting the uttermost farthing, but as a Father, who in grace deals with each one according to his capacity, and accepts the devotion and the intention of the heart.

We understand this of an earthly father. A child of ten is doing some little service for the father, or helping him in his work. The work of the child is very defective, and yet a cause of joy and hope to the father, because he sees in it the proof of the child's attachment and obedience, as well as the pledge of what that spirit will do for the child when his intelligence and his strength have been increased. The child has served the father with a perfect heart, though the perfect heart does not at once imply perfect work.

Even so the Father in heaven accepts as a perfect heart the simple childlike purpose that makes His fear and service its one object. The Christian may be deeply humbled at the involuntary uprisings of the evil nature; but God's Spirit teaches him to say, "It is no more I, but sin that dwelleth in me." He may be sorely grieved by the consciousness of shortcoming and failure, but he hears the voice of Jesus, "The spirit is willing, but the flesh is weak."

Even as Christ counted the love and obedience of His faithless disciples as such, and accepted it as the condition on which He had promised them the Spirit, the Christian can receive the witness of the Spirit that the Father sees and accepts in him the perfect heart, even where there is not yet the perfect performance.[2]

"Thou shalt be perfect with the Lord thy God." Oh! let us beware making the Word of God of none effect by our traditions. Let us believe the message, "Ye are not under the law, but under grace." Let us realize what grace is in its pitying tenderness: "As a father pitieth his children, so the Lord pitieth them that fear him"; what grace is in its mighty power working in us both to will and to do: "The God of all grace shall himself perfect you." If we hold fast our integrity, our confidence, and the rejoicing of hope steadfast unto the end, being perfect in heart will lead us on to be perfect in the way, and we shall realize that Christ fulfills this too in us: "Thou shalt be perfect with the Lord thy God."

CHAPTER FOUR

BE PERFECT!

I Have Walked Before Thee with a Perfect Heart

"Then [Hezekiah] prayed unto the Lord, saying, I beseech Thee, O Lord, remember now how I have walked before thee in truth and with a perfect heart, and have done that which is good in thy sight.... And the word of the Lord came to [Isaiah], saying.... Tell Hezekiah,... Thus saith the Lord, I have heard thy prayer: ... behold, I will heal thee" (II Kings 20: 2–5).

W HAT A CHILDLIKE SIMPLICITY of communion with God! When the Son was about to die, He spake, "I have glorified thee on earth, I have finished the work which thou gavest me to do. And now, O Father, glorify thou me." He pleaded His life and work as the ground for expecting an answer to His prayer. And so Hezekiah, the servant of God, also pleaded, not as a matter of merit, but in the confidence that "God is not unrighteous to forget our work of faith and labour of love," that God should remember how he had walked before Him with a perfect heart.

The words first of all suggest to us this thought, that the man who walks before God with a perfect heart can know it—it may be a matter of consciousness. Let us look at the testimony Scripture gives of him (II Kings 18: 3–6), "He did that which was right in the sight of the Lord, according to all that David his father did." Then follow the different elements of this life that was right in God's sight. "He trusted in the Lord God of Israel. He clave to the Lord. He departed not from following Him. He kept His commandments, which the Lord commanded Moses. And the Lord was with him." His life was one of trust and love, of steadfastness and obedience. And the Lord was with him. He was one of the saints of whom we read, "By faith they obtained a good report." They had the witness that they were righteous, that they were pleasing to God.

Let us seek to have this blessed consciousness. Paul had it when he wrote, "Our glorying is this, the testimony of our conscience, that in holiness and sincerity of God, not in fleshly wisdom, but in the grace of God, we behaved ourselves" (II Cor. 1: 12).

John had it when he said, "Beloved, if our heart condemn us not, we have boldness toward God; and whatever we ask we receive, because we keep his commandments, and do the things that are pleasing in his sight" (I John 3:21, 22). If we are to have perfect peace and confidence, if we are to walk in the holy boldness and the blessed glorying of which Scripture speaks, we must know that our heart is perfect with God.

Hezekiah's prayer suggests a second lesson—that the consciousness of a perfect heart gives wonderful power in prayer. Read over again the words of his prayer, and notice how distinctly this walk with a perfect heart is his plea. Read over again the words just quoted from John, and see how clearly he says that *"because we keep his commandments we receive what we ask."* It is a heart that does not condemn us, that knows that it is perfect toward God, that gives us boldness.

There is most probably not a single reader of these lines who cannot testify how painfully at some time or other the consciousness of the heart not being perfect with God has hindered confidence and prayer. And mistaken views as to what the perfect heart means, and as to the danger of self-righteousness in praying Hezekiah's prayer, have in very many cases banished all idea of its ever being possible to attain to that

boldness and confident assurance of an answer
to prayer which John connects with a heart that
does not condemn us.

Oh! that we would give up all our prejudices,
and learn to take God's Word as it stands as
the only rule of our faith, the only measure of
our expectations. Our daily prayers would be
a new reminder that God asks the perfect heart;
a new occasion of childlike confession as to our
walking or not walking with a perfect heart before God; a new motive to make nothing less
the standard of our communion with our Father
in heaven. How our boldness in God's presence
would be ever clearer; how our consciousness of
His acceptance would be brighter; how the
humbling thought of our nothingness would be
quickened, and our assurance of His strength in
our weakness, and His answer to our prayer,
become the joy of our life.

Oh! the comfort, amid all consciousness of
imperfection of attainment, of being able to
say, in childlike simplicity, "Remember, O Lord,
how I have walked before thee with a perfect
heart."

CHAPTER FIVE

BE PERFECT!

O Lord, Give a Perfect Heart

"Give unto Solomon my son a perfect heart, to keep thy commandments, thy testimonies, and thy statutes" (I Chron. 29:19).

"Let my heart be perfect in thy testimonies" (Ps. 119:80).

IN HIS PARTING COMMISSION to Solomon, David had laid it upon him to serve God with a perfect heart, because He is God who searches the hearts. It is nothing less than the heart, the whole heart, a perfect heart, that God wants. Very shortly afterwards, in his dedication prayer after the giving of all the material for the temple, he turns again to this as the one thing needful, and asks it for his son as a gift from God. "Give my son Solomon a perfect heart."

The perfect heart is a gift from God, given and received under the laws which rule all His giving as a hidden seed to be accepted and acted on in faith. The command "be perfect" comes and claims immediate and full submission. Where this submission is yielded, the need of a divine power to fit for it becomes the motive for urgent and earnest prayer. The word of command, received and hid in a good and honest heart, becomes itself the seed of a divine power.

God works His grace in us by stirring us to work. So the desire to listen to God's command, and to serve Him with a perfect heart, is a beginning that God looks to, and that He himself will strengthen and perfect. The gift of a perfect heart is thus obtained by the obedience of faith. Begin at once to serve God with a perfect heart, and the perfect heart will be given thee.

The perfect heart is a gift from God, to be asked for, to be obtained by prayer. No one will pray for it earnestly, perseveringly, believingly, until he accepts God's Word fully that it is a positive command and an immediate duty to be perfect. Where this has been done, the consciousness will soon grow strong of the utter impossibility of attempting obedience in human strength. And the faith will grow that the word of command was simply meant to draw the soul to Him who gives what He asks.

The perfect heart is a gift to be obtained in

prayer. David asked the Lord to give it to his son Solomon, even as he had prayed for himself long before, "Let my heart be perfect in thy testimonies." Let all of us who long for this blessing follow his example: let us make it a matter of definite, earnest prayer. Let each son and daughter of God say to the Father: "Give Thy child a perfect heart."

Let us in the course of our meditations in this little book turn each word of command, or teaching, or promise into prayer—pointed, personal prayer that asks and claims, that accepts and proves the gift of a perfect heart. And when the seed begins to strike root, and the spirit gives the consciousness that the first beginnings of the perfect heart have been bestowed in the wholehearted purpose to live for God alone, let us hold on in prayer for the perfect heart in all its completeness.

A heart perfect in its purpose towards God— this is only the initial stage. Then there comes the putting on of one grace after another—the going, from strength to strength, on to perfection—the putting on, in ever-growing distinctness of likeness, the Lord Jesus, with every trait of His holy image. All this is to be sought and found in prayer too. It is just he who knows most of what it is to be perfect in purpose who will pray most to be perfect in practice too.

In the words of Hezekiah, we see that there are two elements in the perfect heart: the relation to God, and to His commandments. "I have walked *before thee* with a perfect heart, and *have done* that which is good in thy sight." David speaks of the second of these in his prayer, "a perfect heart to *keep* thy commandments." The two always go together: walking before God will ensure walking in His commandments.

"Every good gift and every perfect gift is from above, coming down from the Father of lights," so is the gift of a perfect heart too. "But let [us] ask in faith, nothing wavering." Let us be sure that in the believing, adoring worship of God there will be given to the soul that is set upon having it, nothing less than what God himself means with a perfect heart. Let us pray the prayer boldly, "Lord, give Thy child a perfect heart. Let my heart be perfect in thy testimonies."

CHAPTER SIX

BE PERFECT!

God's Strength for the Perfect in Heart

"Were not the Ethiopians and the Lubims a huge host? Yet, because thou didst rely on the Lord, he delivered them into thine hand. For the eyes of the Lord run to and fro throughout the whole earth, to show himself strong in the behalf of them whose heart is perfect toward him" (II Chron. 16:8, 9).

WE HAVE HERE the same three thoughts we had in God's words to Abraham. There, it was the command to be perfect in connection with the faith in God's power and a walk in His presence. Here, we have the perfect heart spoken of as the condition of the experience of God's power, and as that which His eyes seek and approve in those who walk before Him. The words teach us the great lesson of the value of the perfect heart in His sight. It is the one thing

He longs for. "His eyes run to and fro throughout the whole earth" to find such. The Father seeketh such to worship Him. And when He finds them, then He shows himself strong in their behalf. It is the one thing that marks the soul as having the capacity of receiving, and showing forth to God's glory, His strength.

The context proves that the chief mark of the perfect heart is trust in God. "Because thou didst rely on the Lord, he delivered them into thine hand. *For* the eyes of the Lord run to and fro ... to show himself strong in behalf of them whose heart is perfect toward him." The essence of faith is this: it gives God His place and glory as God; it allows Him free scope to work, relying on Him alone; it lets God be God. In such faith or reliance the heart proves itself perfect toward God; with no other object of confidence or desire, it depends upon none but Him. As the eyes of God go to and fro throughout the world, wherever He discovers such a man, He delights to prove himself strong to him, to work for him or in him, as the case may be, according to the riches of the glory of His power.

What precious lessons these words teach us for the Christian's life. To have God reveal His strength in us, to have Him make us strong for life or work, for doing or for suffering, *our heart must be perfect with Him*. Let us not shrink from accepting the truth. Let no preconceived opinion as to the impossibility of perfection keep us from allowing the Word of God to have its full effect upon us. He shows himself strong to those whose heart is perfect toward Him. Before we attempt to define exactly, let us first receive the truth that there is such a thing as what God calls a perfect heart, and say it shall be ours. Let us rest content with nothing short of knowing that the eyes of the Lord have seen that we are wholehearted with Him. Let us not be afraid to say, "With my whole heart have I sought thee."

We saw how the chief mark of this perfect heart is reliance upon God. God looks for men who trust Him fully; in them He will show His power. God is a Being of infinite and incomprehensible glory and power. Our mind can form no right conception of what He can do for us. Even when we have His word and promises, our human thoughts of what He means are always defective. By nothing do we dishonor God more than limiting Him. By nothing do we limit Him more than by allowing our human ideas of what He purposes to be the measure of our expectations. The reliance of a heart perfect towards Him is simply this: it yields to Him as God, it rests upon Him, it allows Him, as God, to do in His own way what He has promised.

The heart is perfect towards Him in meeting Him with a perfect faith for all that He is and does as God. Faith expects from God what is beyond all expectation.

The Father seeketh such. Oh! with what joy He findeth them. How He delights in them as His eyes, running to and fro throughout the world, rest upon them to show himself their strong and mighty Helper! Let us walk before this God with a perfect heart, relying upon Him yet to work in us above all that we can ask or think. The one great need of the spiritual life is to know how entirely it is dependent upon God working in us, and what the exceeding greatness of His power is in us who believe. As the soul knows this, and with a perfect heart yields to this Almighty God to let Him do His work within, oh! how strong He will show himself in its behalf.

CHAPTER SEVEN

BE PERFECT!

With the Perfect,
God Shows Himself Perfect

"I was also perfect with him, and I kept my-self from mine iniquity. With the merciful [per-fect] man thou wilt show thyself merciful [per-fect]. As for God, his way is perfect. He is a shield to them that trust him. The God that girdeth me with strength, and maketh my way perfect" (Ps. 18:23, 25, 30, 32).

As FOR GOD, his way is perfect." In all He does, and all He is, God is the perfection of goodness and beauty. In nature and grace, in heaven and on earth, in the greatest and the least, everything that is in God and of God, down to the very hem of His garment, is infinite per-fection. If men who study and admire the perfec-tion of His works, if saints who love and seek the perfection of His service and fellowship, but understood it, they would see that here alone

41

perfection can be truly known and found—in God himself. As for God—this is the highest we can say of Him, though we comprehend but little of it—as for God, His way is perfect.

"He maketh my way perfect." Of God's perfection this is the chief excellence—that He does not keep it for himself: heaven and earth are full of His glory. God is love, who lives, not for himself, but in the energy of an infinite life, makes His creatures, as far as they can possibly receive it, partakers of His perfection. It is His delight to perfect all around Him. And specially the soul of man that rises up to Him. Between His servant and Himself, God would have perfect harmony. The Father wants the child to be as Himself. The more I learn in adoring worship to say, "As for God, his way is perfect," the sooner shall I have faith and grace with the Psalmist to say, "He maketh my way perfect."

As we believe this, that is, receive the heavenly truth in these words into our inmost being and assimilate it, we shall not wonder that the same man also said, *"I was also perfect with him,* and kept myself from mine iniquity." *The God* that girdeth me with strength, and maketh my way perfect": His alone is the power and the honor and the glory of what He hath wrought. This makes the confession, "I was also perfect with him," so far from being presumption or self-righteousness, nothing but an ascription of praise to Him to whom it is due.

And then follow the words in which the perfection of God and that of man are seen in their wonderful relationship and harmony: *"With the perfect man thou wilt show thyself perfect."* As little as there can be a ray of the light of day, however dull and clouded it be, but what speaks of the sun, so little can there be any perfection but what is of God. In its feeblest beginnings in a soul, in its darkest and almost hopeless strugglings, it is all God's perfection wrestling with man to break through and get possession.[3] As long as man refuses to consent, God cannot make His perfection known, for God must be to us what we are to Him: "With the perverse thou wilt show thyself froward." But where man's will consents, and his heart chooses this perfection and this perfect God as its portion, God meets the soul with ever larger manifestations of how perfect He is towards His own. "With the perfect man thou wilt show thyself perfect."

Christian! walk before God with a perfect heart, and you will experience how perfect the heart, and the love, and the will of God to bless, is towards you. Of a heart perfectly yielded to Him, God will take perfect possession. Walk before God in a perfect way—it is God who maketh my way perfect—and your eyes and heart will be opened to see, in adoring wonder, how perfect God's way is with you and for you. Do take mightily hold of this word as the law of God's revelation of himself: "With the perfect man thou wilt show thyself perfect."

To a soul perfectly devoted to Him, God will wonderfully reveal himself. Turn with your whole heart and life, your whole trust and obedience, toward God—walk before Him with a perfect heart—and He will show himself perfect to you, the God whose way is perfect and makes your way perfect, the God who perfects you in every good thing. Meet God with your, "With my whole heart have I sought thee"; He will answer you with His, "Yea, I will rejoice over you to do you good, with my whole heart and with my whole soul." Oh! say it in faith, and hope, and joy. "With the perfect man thou wilt show thyself perfect."

CHAPTER EIGHT

BE PERFECT!

Perfect in Heart Leads to Perfect in the Way

"Blessed are they that are perfect in the way, who walk in the law of the Lord. Blessed are they that keep his testimonies, that seek him with the whole heart" (Ps. 119: 1, 2).

"Let my heart be perfect in thy testimonies" (Ps. 119: 80).

"I will behave myself wisely in a perfect way. Oh! when wilt thou come unto me? I will walk within my house with a perfect heart" (Ps. 101: 2).

W E HAVE SEEN what Scripture says of the perfect heart: here it speaks of the perfect walk. "Blessed are they that are perfect in the way, who walk in the law of the Lord." These are the opening words of the beautiful psalm, in which there is given us the picture, from the witness of personal experience, of the wonder-

ful blessedness of a life in the law and the will
of God. As he looks back upon the past, the
Psalmist does not hesitate to claim that he has
kept that law: "I have kept thy testimonies";
"I have observed thy law"; "I forsook not thy
precepts"; "I have not turned aside from thy
judgments"; "I have done judgment and justice";
"I have not swerved from thy testimonies"; "I
have done thy commandments"; "My soul hath
observed thy testimonies." Of a truth may the
man who can look up to God and, in simplicity
of soul, speak thus, say, "How blessed are the
perfect in the way!"

What is meant by this being "perfect in the
way" becomes plain as we study the psalm.
Perfection includes two elements. The one is the
perfection of heart, the earnestness of purpose,
with which a man gives himself up to seek God
and His will. The other, the perfection of obedience, in which a man seeks, not only to do some,
but all the commandments of his God, and rests
content with nothing less than the New Testament privilege of "standing perfect in all the
will of God." Of both, the Psalmist speaks with
great confidence.

Hear how he testifies of the former in words
such as these: "Blessed are they that seek him
with the whole heart"; "With my whole heart
have I sought thee"; "With my whole heart shall

I observe thy law"; "I will keep thy precepts with my whole heart"; "Thy law is my delight"; "O how love I thy law!" "Consider how I love thy precepts"; "I love them exceedingly."

This is indeed the perfect heart of which we have already heard. The whole psalm is a prayer and an appeal to God himself to consider and see how His servant in wholehearted simplicity has chosen God and His law as his only portion.[4]

We have more than once said that in this wholeheartedness, in the perfect heart, we have the root of all perfection.

But it is only the root and beginning: there is another element that may not be wanting. God is to be found in His will; he who would truly find and fully enjoy God must meet Him in all His will. This is not always understood. A man may have his heart intent on serving God perfectly, and yet may be unconscious how very imperfect his knowledge of God's will is. The very earnestness of his purpose and his consciousness of integrity towards God may deceive him. As far as he knows, he does God's will. But he forgets how much there is of that blessed will that he does not yet know. He can learn a very blessed lesson from the writer of our psalm.

Hear how he speaks: "I have refrained my feet from *every* evil way"; "I hate *every* false way"; "I esteem *all* thy precepts concerning *all* things to be right." It is this surrender to a life of entire and perfect obedience that explains at once the need he felt of divine teaching, and the confidence with which he pleaded for it and expected it: "Let my heart be perfect in thy testimonies." The soul that longs for nothing less than to be perfect in the way, and in deep consciousness of its need of a divine teaching pleads for it, will not be disappointed.

In our next meditation we pass on to the New Testament. In the Old we have the time of preparation, the awakening of the spirit of holy expectancy, waiting God's fulfillment of His promises. In the Old the perfect heart was the vessel, emptied and cleansed for God's filling. In the New we shall find Christ perfected forevermore, perfecting us and fitting us to walk perfect in Him. In the New the word that looks at the human side, *perfect in heart,* disappears to give place to that which reveals the divine filling that waits the prepared vessel: *perfect love—God's love perfected in us.*

"Blessed are they that are perfect in the way!" We have heard the testimony of an Old Testament saint, and is it not written of New Testament times, "He that is feeble shall be as David"?

Surely now, in the fullness of time, when Jesus our High Priest in the power of an endless life saves completely, and the Holy Spirit has come out of God's heaven to dwell within us and be our life, surely now there need not be one word of the psalm that is not meant to be literal truth in the mouth of every believer. Let us read it once more. Speaking it word for word before God, as its writer did, we too shall begin to sing, "Blessed are they that are perfect in the way, ... that seek him with the whole heart."

"I will behave myself wisely in a perfect way. Oh! when wilt thou come unto me? I will walk within my house with a perfect heart."

CHAPTER NINE

BE PERFECT!

Perfect As the Father

"Ye therefore shall be perfect, as your heavenly Father is perfect" (Matt. 5:48).

P ERFECT BEFORE GOD, perfect with God, perfect toward God—these are the expressions we find in the Old Testament. They all indicate a relation: the choice or purpose of the heart set upon God, the wholehearted desire to trust and obey Him. The first word of the New Testament at once lifts us to a very different level, and opens to us what Christ has bought for us. Not only perfect toward God, but—*perfect as God*. This is the wonderful prospect it holds out to us. It reveals the infinite fullness of meaning the word perfect has in God's mind. It gives us at once the only standard we are to aim at and to judge by. It casts down all hopes of perfection as a human attainment; but wakens hope in Him who, as God, has the power, as Father has the will, to make us like himself.

A young child may be the perfect image of his father. There may be a great difference in age, in stature, in power, and yet the resemblance may be so striking that everyone notices it. And so a child of God, though infinitely less, may yet bear the image of the Father so markedly, may have such a striking likeness to his Father, that in his creaturely life he shall be perfect as the Father is in His divine life. This is possible. It is what Jesus here commands. It is what each one should aim at. "Perfect as your Father in heaven" is perfect," must become one of the first articles of our creed, one of the guiding lights of our Christian life.

Wherein this perfection of the Father consists is evident from the context: "Love your enemies, that ye may be sons of your Father which is in heaven; for he maketh his sun to shine on the evil and the good. Be ye therefore perfect, as your Father in heaven is perfect." Or as it is in Luke 6:36: "Be ye merciful, even as your Father is merciful." The perfection of God is His love; His will to communicate His own blessedness to all around Him. His compassion and mercy are the glory of His being. He created us in His image and after His likeness, to find our glory in a life of love and mercy and beneficence. It is in love we are to be perfect, even as our Father is perfect.

The thought that comes up at once, and that ever returns again, is this: But is it possible? And if so, how? Certainly not as a fruit of man's efforts. But the words themselves contain the answer: "perfect as *your heavenly Father* is perfect."

It is because the little child has received his life from his father, and because the father watches over his training and development, that there can be such a striking and ever-increasing resemblance between him in his feebleness and the father in His strength. It is because the sons of God are partakers of the divine nature, have God's life, and Spirit, and love within them, that the command is reasonable, and its obedience in ever-increasing measure possible: Be perfect, as your Father is.

The perfection is our Father's: we have its seed in us; He delights to give the increase. The words that first appear to cast us down in utter helplessness now become our hope and strength. Be perfect, as *your Father* is perfect. Claim your child's heritage; give up yourself to be wholly a son of God, yield yourself to the Father to do in you all He is able.

And then, remember too, who it is gives this message from the Father. It is the Son, who himself was, by the Father, perfected through suffering; who learned obedience and was made perfect; and who has perfected us forever. The message "be perfect" comes to us from Him, our elder Brother, as a promise of infinite hope.

What Jesus asks of us, the Father gives. What Jesus speaks, He does. To "present every man perfect in Christ Jesus" is the one aim of Christ and His gospel. Let us accept the command from Him; in yielding ourselves to obey it, let us yield ourselves to Him: let our expectation be from Him in whom we have been perfected. Through faith in Him we receive the Holy Ghost, by whom the love of God is shed abroad in our heart. Through faith in Him that love becomes in us a fountain of love springing up without ceasing. In union with Him the love of God is perfected in us, and we are perfected in love. Let us not fear to accept and obey the command, "Be perfect, as your heavenly Father is perfect."

CHAPTER TEN

BE PERFECT!

Perfected As the Master

"Be ye therefore merciful, as your Father also is merciful. . . . The disciple is not above his master: but every one when he is perfected shall be as his master" (Luke 6: 36, 40).

IN HIS REPORT of part of the Sermon on the Mount, Luke records that Jesus says, not: Be perfect, but, Be merciful, as your Father is. He then introduces the word perfect immediately after; not, however, in connection with the Father, but the Son, as the Master of His disciples. The change is most instructive; it leads us to look to Jesus, as He dwelt in the flesh, as our model.

It might be said that our circumstances and powers are so different from those of God that it is impossible to apply the standard of His infinite perfection in our little world. But here comes the Son, in the likeness of sinful flesh, tempted in all things like as we are, and offers himself as our Master and Leader. He lives with us that we may live with Him; He lives like us that we may live like Him.

The divine standard is embodied and made visible, is brought within our reach, in the human model. Growing into His likeness, who is the image of the Father, we shall bear the likeness of the Father too: becoming like Him, the first-born among many brethren, we shall become perfect as the Father is. "The disciple is not above his master: but every one when he is perfected shall be as his master."

"The disciple is not above his master." The thought of the disciple being as the Master sometimes has reference to outward humiliation: like the Master he will be despised and persecuted (Matt. 10:24, 25; John 15:20). And sometimes to inward humility, the willingness to be a servant (Luke 22:27; John 13:16). Both in his external life and his inner disposition the perfected disciple knows nothing higher than to be as his Master.

To take Jesus as Master, with the distinct desire and aim to be and live and act like Him—this is true Christianity. This is something far more than accepting Him as a Saviour and Helper; far more even than acknowledging Him as Lord and Master.

A servant may obey the commands of his master most faithfully, while he has little thought of through them rising up into the master's likeness and spirit. This alone is full discipleship, to long in everything to be as like the Master as possible, to count His life as the true expression of all that is perfect, and to aim at nothing less than the perfection of being perfect as He was. "Every one when he is perfected shall be as his master."

The words suggest to us very distinctly that in discipleship there is more than one stage. Just as in the Old Testament it is said only of some that they served the Lord with a perfect heart, while of others we read that their heart was not perfect with the Lord (I Kings 11:4, 15: 3; II Chron. 25:2), so even now there are great differences between disciples. Some there are to whom the thought of aiming at the perfect likeness of the Master has never come: they only look to Christ as a Saviour. And some there are whose heart indeed longs for full conformity to their Lord, "to be as the master," but who have never understood, though they have read the words, that there is such a thing as "a perfect heart" and a life "perfected in love."

But there are those, too, to whom it has been given to accept these words in their divine meaning and truth, and who do know in blessed experience what it is to say with Hezekiah, "I have walked before thee with a perfect heart," and with John, "As he is, even so are we in this world."

As we go on in our study of what Scripture says of perfection, let us hold fast the principle we have learned here. Likeness to Jesus in His humiliation and humility: the choice, like Him, of the form of a servant, the spirit that does not exercise lordship and would not be ministered unto, but girds itself to minister and to give its life for others—this is the secret of true perfection. "The disciple is not above his master, but every one when he is perfected shall be as his master." With the perfect love of God as our standard, with that love revealed in Christ's humanity and humility as our model and guide, with the Holy Spirit to strengthen us with might, that this Christ may live in us, we shall learn to know what it is that everyone who when he is perfected shall be as his Master.

CHAPTER ELEVEN

BE PERFECT!

The Perfect Selling All to Follow Christ

"Jesus said unto him, If thou wouldest be perfect, go, sell that which thou hast, and give to the poor, and thou shalt have treasure in heaven: and come, follow me" (Matt. 19:21).

To the rich young ruler poverty was to be the path to perfection. "The disciple is not above his master, but every one when he is perfected shall be as his master." Poverty was part of the Master's perfection, part of that mysterious discipline of self-denial and suffering through which it became God to perfect Him: while He was on earth poverty was to be the mark of all those who would be always with, wholly as, the Master.

What does this mean? Jesus was Lord of all. He might have lived here on earth in circumstances of comfort and with moderate possessions. He might have taught us how to own, and to use, and to sanctify property. He might in this have become like us, walking in the path in which most men have to walk. But He chose poverty. Its life of self-sacrifice and direct dependence on God, its humiliation, its trials and temptations, were to be elements of that highest perfection He was to exhibit.

In the disciples whom He chose to be with Him poverty was to be the mark of their fellowship with Him, the training school for perfect conformity to His image, the secret of power for victory over the world, for the full possession of the heavenly treasure, and the full exhibition of the heavenly spirit. And even in him, who, when the humiliation was past, had his calling from the throne, in Paul, poverty was still the chosen and much-prized vehicle of perfect fellowship with his Lord.

What does this mean? The command "be perfect" comes to the rich as well as the poor. Scripture has nowhere spoken of the possession of property as a sin. While it warns against the danger riches bring, and denounces their abuse, it has nowhere promulgated a law forbidding riches. And yet it speaks of poverty as having a very high place in the life of perfection.

To understand this we must remember that

perfection is a relative term. We are not under a law, with its external commands as to duty and conduct, that takes no account of diversity of character or circumstance. In the perfect law of liberty in which we are called to live, there is room for infinite variety in the manifestation of our devotion to God and Christ.

According to the diversity of gifts and circumstances and calling, the same spirit may be seen in apparently conflicting paths of life. There is a perfection which is sought in the right possession and use of earthly goods as the Master's steward; there is also a perfection which seeks even in external things to be as the Master himself was, and in poverty to bear its witness to the reality and sufficiency of heavenly things.

In the early ages of the Church this truth, that poverty is for some the path of perfection, exercised a mighty and blessed influence. Men felt that poverty, as one of the traits of the holy life of Jesus and His apostles, was sacred and blessed. As the inner life of the Church grew feeble, the spiritual truth was lost in external observances, and the fellowship of the poverty of Jesus was scarce to be seen. In its protest against the self-righteousness and the superficiality of the Romish system, the Protestant Church has not yet been able to give to poverty the place it ought to have either in the portraiture of the Master's image or the disciples' study of perfect conformity to Him.

And yet it is a truth many are seeking after. If our Lord found poverty the best school for His own strengthening in the art of perfection, and the surest way to rise above the world and win men's hearts for the Unseen, it surely need not surprise us if those who feel drawn to seek the closest possible conformity to their Lord even in external things, and who long for the highest possible power in witnessing for the Invisible, should be irresistibly drawn to count this word as spoken to them too: "If thou wouldest be perfect, go, sell that which thou hast, and . . . follow me."

When this call is not felt, there is a larger lesson of universal application: No perfection without the sacrifice of all. To be perfected here on earth Christ gave up all: to become like Him, to be perfected as the Master, means the giving up of all. The world and self must be renounced. "If thou wouldest be perfect, go, sell that which thou hast, and give to the poor, . . . and come, follow me."

CHAPTER TWELVE

BE PERFECT!

The Perfect Man a Spiritual Man

"Howbeit we speak wisdom among them that are perfect" (I Cor. 2:6).

"And I, brethren, could not speak unto you as unto spiritual, but as unto carnal, as unto babes in Christ. . . . For whereas there is among you jealousy and strife, are ye not carnal?" (I Cor. 3:1, 3).

AMONG THE CORINTHIANS there were mighty and abundant operations of the Holy Spirit. Paul could say to them, "In everything ye were enriched in Christ, so that ye come behind in no gift" (I Cor. 1:5). And yet in the sanctifying grace of the Holy Spirit there was much that was wanting. He had to say, "There are contentions among you; I beseech you that there be no divisions among you, but that ye may be *perfected together* in the same mind."

The spirit of humility, and gentleness, and

unity was wanting; without these they could not be perfected, either individually or as a body. They needed the injunction, "Above all these things put on love, which is the bond of perfectness."

The Corinthians were as yet carnal; the gifts of the Spirit were among them in power; but His grace, renewing, sweetening, sanctifying every temper into the likeness of Jesus, in this they were lacking much. The wisdom Paul preached was a heavenly, spiritual wisdom: "God's wisdom is a mystery, even the hidden wisdom," which needed a spiritual, heavenly mind to apprehend it. "We speak wisdom among them that are perfect"; he could not speak to them "as unto spiritual, but as unto carnal."

Spiritual things must be spiritually discerned; the wisdom among the perfect could only be received by those who were not carnal, but spiritual. The perfect of whom Paul speaks are the spiritual.

And who are the spiritual? Those in whom not only the gifts, but the graces of the Spirit have obtained supremacy and are made manifest. God's love is His perfection (Matt. 5: 40–46); Christ's humility is His perfection. The self-sacrificing love of Christ, His humility, and meekness, and gentleness, manifested in daily life, are the most perfect fruit of the Spirit, the true proof that a man is spiritual.

A man may have great zeal in God's service, he may be used to influence many for good, and yet, weighed in the balance of love, be found sadly wanting. In the heat of controversy, or under unjust criticism, haste of temper, slowness to forgive and forget, quick words and sharp judgments, often reveal an easily wounded sensitiveness, which proves how little the Spirit of Christ has full possession or real mastery. The spiritual man is the man who is clothed with the spirit of the suffering, crucified Jesus.

And it is only the spiritual man who can understand "the wisdom among the perfect," "even the mystery which now hath been manifested to the holy ones, to whom God was pleased to make known what is the riches of the glory of this mystery, which is Christ in you."

A Christian teacher may be a man of wonderful sagacity and insight, may have the power of opening the truth, of mightily stimulating and helping others, and may yet have so much of the carnal that the deeper mystery of Christ in us remains hidden. It is only as we yield ourselves wholly to the power of God's Holy Spirit, as the question of being made free from all that is carnal, of attaining the utmost possible likeness to Jesus in His humiliation, of being filled with the Spirit, rules heart and life, that the Christian, be he scholar or teacher, can fully enter into the wisdom among the perfect.

To know the mind of God we must have the mind of Christ. And the mind of Christ is this, that He emptied and humbled himself, and became obedient to death. This humility was His capacity, His fitness for rising to the throne of God. This mind must be in us if the hidden wisdom of God is to be revealed to us in its power. This is the mark of the spiritual, the perfect man.

May God increase the number of the perfect. And to that end the number of those who know to speak wisdom among the perfect, even God's wisdom in a mystery. As the distinction between the carnal and the spiritual, the babes and the perfect, comes to recognition in the Church, the connection between a spiritual life and spiritual insight will become clearer, and the call to perfection will gain new force and meaning. And it will once again be counted just cause of reproof and of shame not to be among the perfect.

CHAPTER THIRTEEN

BE PERFECT!

Perfecting Holiness

"Having therefore these promises, beloved, let us cleanse ourselves from all defilement of flesh and spirit, perfecting holiness in the fear of God" (II Cor. 7:1).

THESE WORDS GIVE US AN INSIGHT into one of the chief aspects of perfection, and an answer to the question, Wherein is it we are to be perfect? We must be perfect in holiness. We must be perfectly holy. Such is the exposition of the Father's message, be perfect.

We know what holiness is. God alone is holy, and holiness is that which God communicates of himself. Separation and cleansing and consecration are not holiness, but only the preliminary steps on the way to it. The temple was holy because God dwelt in it. Not that which is given to God is holy, but that which God accepts and appropriates, that which He takes possession of, takes up into His own fellowship and use—that is holy. "I am the Lord which makes you holy," was God's promise to His people of old, on which the command was based, "Be ye holy." God's taking them for His own made them a holy people; their entering into this holiness of God, yielding themselves to His will and fellowship and service, was what the command "Be ye holy" called them to.

Even so it is with us Christians. We are made holy in Christ; we are saints or holy ones. The call comes to us to follow after holiness to perfect holiness, to yield ourselves to the God who is ready to sanctify us wholly. It is the knowledge of what God has done in making us His holy ones, and has promised to do in sanctifying us wholly, that will give us courage to perfect holiness.

"Having therefore these promises, beloved, let us . . . [perfect] holiness." Which promises? They had just been mentioned: "I will dwell in them; I will be their God; I will receive you; I will be to you a Father." It was God's accepting the temple and dwelling there himself that made it holy. It is God's dwelling in us that makes us holy, that gives us not only the motive, but the courage and the power to perfect holiness, to yield ourselves for Him to possess perfectly and entirely. It is God's being a father to us, begetting His own life, His own Son within us, forming Christ in us, until the Son and the Father make their abode in us, that will give us confidence to believe that it is possible to perfect holiness, and will reveal to us the secret of its attainment. "Having therefore these promises, beloved," that is, knowing them, living on them, claiming and obtaining them, let us "perfect holiness."

This faith is the secret power of the growth of the inner life of perfect holiness. But there are hindrances that check and prevent this growth. These must be watched against and removed. "Having these promises, . . . let us cleanse ourselves from all defilement of flesh and spirit, perfecting holiness in the fear of the Lord." Every defilement, outward or inward, in conduct or sentiment, in the physical or the spiritual life, must be cleansed and cast away. Cleansing in the blood, cleansing by the Word, cleansing by the pruningknife or the fire—in any way or by any means—but we must be cleansed. In the fear of the Lord every sin must be cut off and cast out; everything doubtful or defiling must be put away; soul and body and spirit must be preserved entire and blameless. Thus cleansing ourselves from all defilement we shall perfect holiness: the spirit of holiness will fill God's temple with His holy presence and power.

Beloved, having these promises, let us perfect holiness. Perfectly holy! perfect in holiness!— let us yield ourselves to these thoughts, to these wishes, to these promises, of our God. Beginning with the perfect childlike heart, pressing on in the perfect way, clinging to a perfect Saviour, living in fellowship with a God whose way and work is perfect, let us not be afraid to come to God with His own command as our prayer: "Perfect holiness, O my Lord!" He knows what He means by it, and we shall know if we follow on to know.

"Lord, I am called to perfect holiness: I come to Thee for it; make me as perfectly holy as a redeemed sinner can be on earth."

Let this be the spirit of our daily prayer: I would walk before God with a perfect heart— perfect in Christ Jesus; in the path of perfect holiness. I would this day come as near perfection as grace can make it possible for me. "Perfecting holiness" shall, in the power of His Spirit, be my aim.

CHAPTER FOURTEEN

BE PERFECT!

We Pray for Your Perfecting: Be Perfected

"This we also pray for, even your perfecting... Finally, brethren, farewell. Be perfected; be comforted; be of the same mind; live in peace: and the God of love and peace shall be with you" (II Cor. 13:9, 11).

THE WORD HERE TRANSLATED PERFECT means to bring a thing into its right condition, so that it is as it should be.[5] It is used of mending nets, restoring them to their right state, or of equipping a ship: fitting it out with all it should have. It implies thus two things: the removal of all that is still wrong; the supply of all that is still wanting.

Within two verses Paul uses the word twice. First, as the expression of the one thing which he asks of God for them, the summary of all

grace and blessing: "This we pray for, even
your perfecting." That you be perfectly free
from all that is wrong and carnal, and that
you should perfectly possess and exhibit all that
God would have you be: we pray for your perfecting.

Next, as the summing up in a farewell word
of what He would have them aim at, Jesus says:
"Finally, brethren, farewell. Be perfected." And
then follow three other verbs which show how
this one which takes the lead has reference
to the Christian's daily life, and is meant to
point to what is to be his daily aim and experience. "Be perfected; be comforted; be of the
same mind: live in peace."

Just as the comfort of the Spirit and the
unity of love and the life of peace are, if the
God of love and peace is to be with us, our duty
and our privilege every hour, so, too, the being
perfected. The close of the two epistles gathers
up all its teaching in this one injunction: "Farewell. *Be perfected!*"

The two texts together show us what the
prayer and the preaching of every minister of
the gospel ought to be; what his heart, above
everything, ought to be set on. We justly look
upon Paul as a model whom every minister
ought to copy. Let every gospel minister copy
him in this, so that his people may know as he

goes in and out among them that his heart breathes heavenward for them this one wish: your perfecting! and may feel that all his teaching has this one aim: be perfected!

If ministers are to seek this above everything in their charge of the Church of God, they themselves need to feel deeply and to expose faithfully the low standard that prevails in the Church. Some have said that they have seen perfectionism slay its thousands. All must admit that imperfectionism has slain its tens of thousands. Multitudes are soothing themselves in a life of worldliness and sin with the thought that as no one is perfect, imperfection cannot be so dangerous. Numbers of true Christians are making no progress because they have never known that we can serve God with a perfect heart, that the perfect heart is the secret of a perfect way, of a work going on unto perfection.

God's call to us to be perfect—to perfect holiness in His fear, to live perfect in Christ Jesus, to stand perfect in all the will of God—must be preached until the faith begins to live again in the Church that all teaching is to be summed up in the words, and each day of our life to be spent under their inspiration: be perfected!

When once ministers know themselves and

are known as the messengers of this God-willed
perfection, they will feel the need of nothing
less than the teaching of the Holy Spirit to guide
men in this path. They will see and preach that
religion must indeed be a surrender of all to
God. Becoming as conformed to His will, living
as entirely to His glory, being as perfectly devoted to His service, as grace can enable us to
be, and no less, will be the only rule of duty and
measure of expectation.

The message "be perfected!" will demand the
whole heart, the whole life, the whole strength.
As the soul learns each day to say, "Father! I
would be perfect in heart with Thee this day,
I would walk before Thee and be perfect," the
need and the meaning of abiding in Christ will
be better understood; Christ himself with His
power and love will have new preciousness; and
God will prove what He can do for souls, for a
Church, wholly given up to Him.

O ye ministers of Christ, ye messengers of
His salvation, say to the churches over which
the Holy Spirit hath made you overseers: "This
also we pray for—even *your perfecting!* Finally,
brethren, *be perfected!*"

CHAPTER FIFTEEN

BE PERFECT!

Not Perfected, Yet Perfect

"Not that I have already obtained, or am already made perfect [perfected]; but I press on. ... One thing I do, ... I press on toward the goal. ... Let us therefore, as many as are perfect, be thus minded" (Phil. 3: 12–15) .

IN PERFECTION THERE ARE DEGREES. We have perfect, more perfect, most perfect. We have perfect, waiting to be perfected. So it was with our Lord Jesus. In Hebrews we read thrice of Him that He was perfected or made perfect. Of sinful imperfection there was not the faintest shadow in Him. At each moment of His life He was perfect—just what He should be. And yet He needed, and it became God to perfect Him through suffering and the obedience He learned in it. As He conquered temptation, and maintained His allegiance to God, and amid strong crying and tears gave up His will to God's will,

His human nature was perfected, and He became a High Priest, "the Son perfected for evermore." Jesus during His life on earth was perfect but not yet perfected.

"The perfected disciple shall be as his master." What is true of Him is true, in our measure, of us too. Paul wrote to the Corinthians of speaking wisdom among the perfect, a wisdom carnal Christians could not understand. Here in our text he classes himself with the perfect, and expects and enjoins them to be of the same mind with himself. He sees no difficulty either in speaking of himself and others as perfect, or in regarding the perfect as needing to be yet further and fully perfected.

And what is now this perfection which has yet to be perfected? And who are these perfect ones? The man who has made the highest perfection his choice, and who has given his whole heart and life to attain to it, is counted by God a perfect man.

"The kingdom of heaven is like a seed." Where God sees in the heart the single purpose to be all that God wills, He sees the divine seed of all perfection. And as He counts faith for righteousness, so He counts this wholehearted purpose to be perfect as incipient perfection. The man with a perfect heart is accepted by God, amid all imperfection of attainment, as a perfect man. Paul could look upon the Church and un-hesitatingly say, "Let us therefore, as many as are perfect, be thus minded."

We know how among the Corinthians he de-scribes two classes: the one, the large majority, carnal and content to live in strife; the other, the spiritual, the perfect. In the Church of our day it is to be feared that the great majority of believers have no conception of their calling to be perfect. They have not the slightest idea that it is their duty not only to be religious but to be as eminently religious, as full of grace and holiness, as it is possible for God to make them. Even where there is some measure of earnest purpose in the pursuit of holiness, there is such a want of faith in the earnestness of God's purpose when He speaks, "Be perfect," and in the sufficiency of His grace to meet the demand, that the appeal meets with no response. In no real sense do they understand or accept Paul's invitation: "Let us therefore, as many as are perfect, be thus minded."

But, thank God! it is not so with all. There is an ever-increasing number who cannot forget that God means what He says when He speaks "Be perfect," and who regard themselves as un-der the most solemn obligation to obey the command. The words of Christ "be perfect" are to them a revelation of what Christ is come to give and to work, a promise of the blessing to which His teaching and leading will bring them. They have joined the band of like-minded ones whom Paul would associate with himself. They seek God with their whole heart; they serve Him with a perfect heart; their one aim in life is to be made perfect, even as the Master.

My reader! as in the presence of God, who has said to you, "Be perfect!" and of Christ Jesus, who gave himself that you might obey this command of your God, I charge you that you do not refuse the call of God's servant, but enroll yourself among those who accept it: "Let us therefore, as many as are perfect, be thus minded."

Fear not to take your place before God with Paul among the perfect in heart. So far will it be from causing self-complacency that you will learn from him how the perfect has yet to be perfected, and how the one mark of the perfect is that he counts all things loss as he presses on unto the prize of the high calling of God in Jesus Christ.

CHAPTER SIXTEEN

BE PERFECT!

Perfect, and Yet to Be Perfected

"Not that I have already obtained, or am already made perfect [perfected], but I press on. ... One thing I do, ... I press on toward the goal. ... Let us therefore, as many as are perfect, be thus minded. ... Brethren, be ye imitators together of me" (Phil. 3:12–17).

THE MARK OF THE PERFECT, as set before us in Paul and all who are thus minded, is the passionate desire to be yet made perfect. This looks like a paradox. And yet what we see in our Master proves the truth of what we say: the consciousness of being perfect is in entire harmony with the readiness to sacrifice life itself for the sake of being yet made perfect. It was thus with Christ. It was thus with Paul. It will be thus with us, as we open our hearts fully and give God's words room and time to do their work.

Many think that the more imperfect one is the more he will feel his need of perfection. All experience, in every department of life, teaches us the very opposite. It is those who are nearest perfection who most know their need of being yet perfected, and are most ready to make any sacrifice to attain to it. To count everything loss for perfection in practice is the surest proof that perfection in principle has possession of the heart. The more honestly and earnestly the believer claims that he seeks God with a perfect heart, the more ready will he be with Paul to say: "Not that I have already obtained, or am already made perfect."

And wherein was it now that Paul longed to be made perfect? Read the wonderful passage with care and without prejudice or preconceived ideas, and I think you will see that he gives *here* no indication of its being sin or sinful imperfection from which he was seeking to be perfectly free. Whatever his writings teach elsewhere, the thought is not in his mind here. The perfected disciple is as his Master.

Paul is speaking here of his life and lifework, and feels that that is not perfected until he has reached the goal and obtained the prize. To this he is pressing on. He that runs in a race may, as far as he has gone, have done everything perfectly; all may pronounce his course perfect as far as it has gone. Still it has to be perfected. The contrast is not with failure or shortcoming, but with what is as yet unfinished and waiting for its full end.

Paul uses expressions which all tell us that what he already had of Christ was but a part. He did know Christ, he had gained Christ, he was found in Him, he had apprehended in wonderful measure that for which Christ had apprehended him. And yet of all these things—of knowing Christ, of gaining Him, of being found in Him, of apprehending that for which he was apprehended—he speaks as of what he was striving after with all his might: "If by any means I may attain to the resurrection of the dead"; "I press on to the goal, unto the prize." It is of all this he says: "Not that I am already made perfect. Let as many as are perfect be thus minded."

Paul had known Christ for many years, but he knew there were in Him riches and treasures greater than he had known yet, and nothing could satisfy him but the full and final and eternal possession of what the resurrection would bring him. For this he counted all things but loss; for this he forgot the things that were behind; for this he pressed on to the goal, unto the prize. He teaches us the spirit of true perfection. A man who knows he is perfect with God; a man who knows he must yet be perfected; a man who knows that he has counted all things loss to attain this final perfection—such is the perfect man.

Christian, learn here the price of perfection as well as the mark of the perfect ones. The Master gave His life to be made perfect forever. Paul did the same. It is a solemn thing to profess the pursuit of perfection. The price of the pearl of great price is high: all things must be counted loss.

I have urged you to put down your names in the class-list of the perfect; to ask the Master to put it down and give you the blessed witness of the Spirit to a perfect heart. I urge you now, if, like Paul, you claim to be perfect, single and wholehearted in your surrender to God, to live the life of the perfect, with *all things loss for Jesus* as its watchword and its strength, and one desire to possess Him wholly, to be possessed of Him, and to be made perfect even as He was.

"O our Father! be pleased to open the eyes of Thy children that they may see what the perfection of heart is Thou dost now ask of them, and what the perfection in Christ Thou wouldst have them seek at any cost."

CHAPTER SEVENTEEN

BE PERFECT!

Perfect in Christ

"Christ in you, the hope of glory: whom we proclaim, admonishing every man, and teaching every man in all wisdom; that we may present every man perfect in Christ: whereunto I labour also, striving according to his working which worketh in me mightily" (Col. 1:27–29).

PERFECT IN CHRIST: in our inquiry into the teaching of the Word as to perfection, we have here a new word opening up to us the hope, giving us the assurance, of what we have seen to be our duty. It links all that we have seen of God's call and claim with all that we know of Christ in His grace and power. Perfect in Christ: here is the open gateway into the perfect life. He to whom it is given to see fully what it means, finds through it an abundant entrance into the life of Christian perfectness.

There are three aspects in which we need

to look at the truth of our being perfect in Christ. There is, first, our perfectness in Christ, *as it is prepared for us in Him our Head.* As the second Adam, Christ came and wrought out a new nature for all the members of His body. This nature is His own life, perfected through suffering and obedience.

In thus being perfected himself, He perfected forever them that are sanctified. His perfection, His perfect life, is ours not only judicially, or by imputation, but as an actual spiritual reality in virtue of our real and living union with Him. Paul says in the same Epistle, "Ye are complete, made full in him." All that you are to be is already fulfilled, and so you are fulfilled in Him— circumcised in Him, buried with Him, raised with Him, quickened together with Him. All Christ's members are in Him, fulfilled in Him.

Then there is our perfection in Christ as *imparted to us by the Holy Spirit in uniting us to Him.* The life which is implanted in us at the new birth, planted into the midst of a mass of sin and flesh, is a perfect life. As the seed contains in itself the whole life of the tree, so the seed of God within us is the perfect life of Christ, with its power to grow and fill our life and bring forth fruit to perfection.

And then there is also our perfection in Christ *as wrought in us by the Holy Spirit, appropriated*

by us in the obedience of faith, and made mani-
fest in our life and conduct. As our faith grasps
and feeds upon the truth in the two former aspects, and yields itself to God to have that perfect life master and pervade the whole of our
daily life in its ordinary actions—*perfect in*
Christ will become each moment a present practical reality and experience.

All that the Word has taught of the perfect
heart and the perfect way, of being perfect as
the Father and perfect as the Master, shines with
new meaning and with the light of a new life.
Christ, the living Christ, is our perfection. He
himself lives each day and hour to impart it.
The measureless love of Jesus and the power of
the endless life in which His life works become
the measure of our expectation. In the life in
which we now live in the flesh, with its daily
duties in contact with men and money, with care
and temptation, we are to give the proof that
perfect in Christ is no mere ideal, but in the
power of Almighty God, simple and literal truth.

It is in the last of these three aspects that
Paul has used the expression in our text. He
speaks of admonishing every man and teaching
every man in all wisdom that he may present
every man perfect in Christ Jesus. It is to the
perfectness in daily life and walk that the admonishing and teaching have reference.

In principle, Christians were perfect in Christ: in practice they were to become perfect. The aim of the gospel ministry among believers was to present every man perfect in Christ Jesus, to teach men how they might put on the Lord Jesus, have His life cover them and have His life in them.

What a task! What a hopeless task to the minister, as he looks upon the state of the Church! What a task of infinite hopefulness, if he does his work as Paul did, "whereunto," nothing less than *presenting every man perfect in Christ*: "Whereunto I also labour, striving according to his working which worketh in me mightily." The aim is high, but the power is divine. Let the minister, in full purpose of heart, make Paul's aim his own: to present every man perfect in Christ Jesus. He may count upon Paul's strength: "His working which worketh in me mightily."

CHAPTER EIGHTEEN

BE PERFECT!

Perfect in All the Will of God

"Epaphras, who is one of you, a servant of Christ Jesus, saluteth you, always striving for you in his prayers, that ye may stand perfect and fully assured in all the will of God" (Col. 4:12).

IN THIS, as in some of the other Epistles, there is set before us the life of the believer as he lives it in heaven in Christ and then as he lives it here on earth with men. The teaching of Scripture is intensely spiritual and supernatural, but, at the same time, intensely human and practical. This comes out very beautifully in the two expressions of our Epistle. Paul had told the Colossians what he labored for. He now tells them what another minister, Epaphras, asked on their behalf. Paul's *striving* was in his labor that they might be *perfect in Christ Jesus.* The *striving* of Epaphras was in the prayer that they might be *perfect in all the will of God.*

First we have "perfect in Christ Jesus." The
thought is so unearthly and divine that its full
meaning eludes our grasp. It lifts us up to life in
Christ and heaven. Then we have "perfect in
all the will of God." This word brings us down
to earth and daily life, placing all under the
rule of God's will, and calling us in every action
and disposition to live in the will of God.

"That ye may stand perfect in all the will of
God." "The perfection of the creature consists
in nothing but willing the will of the Creator."
The will of God is the expression of the divine
perfection. Nature has its beauty and glory in
being the expression of the divine will. The
angels have their place and bliss in heaven in
doing God's will. The Son of God was perfected
in learning obedience, in giving himself up unto
the will of God. His redemption has but one
object: to bring man into that only place of rest
and blessedness—the will of God.

The prayer of Epaphras shows how truly he
had entered into the spirit of his Master. He
prays for his people that they may stand *in the
will of God;* and that in *all* the will of God—
nothing in their life excepted, in which they
were not in God's will; and that again, *perfect*
in all the will of God, at each moment, with a
perfect heart walking in a perfect way. Perfect
in all the will of God is ever his one thought of

what ought to be asked and could be found in prayer.

Paul prayed for the Colossians "that they might be filled with *the knowledge of God's will* in all wisdom and spiritual understanding." These two servants of God were of one mind: that young converts must be reminded that their knowledge of God's will is very defective, that they need to pray for a divine teaching to know that will, and that their one aim should be to stand perfect in all that will.

Let all seekers after perfection, let all who would be like-minded with Paul, note well the lesson. In the joy of a consecration sealed by the Holy Spirit, in the consciousness of a whole-hearted purpose and of serving God with a perfect heart, the believer is often tempted to forget how much there may be in which he does not yet see God's will. There may be grave defects in his character, serious shortcomings from the law of perfect love in his conduct, which others can observe. The consciousness of acting up to the full light of what we know to be right is a most blessed thing, one of the marks of the perfect heart. But it must ever be accompanied with the remembrance of how much there may be that has not yet been revealed to us.

This sense of ignorance as to much of God's will, this conviction that there is still much in us that needs to be changed and sanctified and perfected will make us very humble and tender, very watchful and hopeful in prayer. So far from interfering with our consciousness that we serve God with a perfect heart, it will give it new strength, while it cultivates that humility which is the greatest beauty of perfection. Without it, the appeal to the consciousness of our uprightness becomes superficial and dangerous, and the doctrine of perfection a stumblingblock and a snare.

Perfect in all the will of God. Let this be our unceasing aim and prayer. Striking its roots deep in the humility which comes from the conviction of how much there is yet to be revealed to us; strengthened by the consciousness that we have given ourselves to serve Him with a perfect heart; full of the glad purpose to be content with nothing less than standing perfect in all the will of God; rejoicing in the confidence of what God will do for those who are before Him perfect in Christ Jesus—let our faith claim the full blessing. God will reveal to us how *perfect in Christ Jesus* and *perfect in all the will of God* are one in His thought, and may be so in our experience.

Paul prayed without ceasing for the Colossians that they might be filled with the knowledge of God's will. Epaphras was always striving in his prayers for them that they might stand perfect in all the will of God.

It is by prayer, by unceasing striving in prayer, that this grace must be sought for the Church. It is before the throne, it is in the presence of God, that the life of perfection must be found and lived. It is by the operation of the mighty quickening power of God himself, waited for and received in prayer, that believers can indeed stand perfect in all the will of God. God give us grace to seek and so to find it.

CHAPTER NINETEEN

BE PERFECT!

Christ Made Perfect Through Suffering

"It became him, ... to make the author [leader] of their salvation perfect through sufferings" (Heb. 2:10).

"Though he was a Son, yet learned he obedience by the things which he suffered; and having been made perfect [perfected], he became unto all them that obey him the author of eternal salvation" (Heb. 5:8, 9).

"But the word of the oath appointeth a Son, perfected for evermore" (Heb. 7:28).

W E HAVE HERE three passages in which we are taught that Jesus Christ himself, though He was the Son of God, had to be perfected. The first tells us that it was as the Leader of our salvation that He was perfected; that it was God's work to perfect Him; that there was a need for it; "it became God" to do it; and that it was through suffering the work was accomplished.

The second passage tells that the power of suffering to perfect was that in it He learned obedience to God's will; and that, being thus perfected, He became the Author of eternal salvation to all who obey Him.

The third passage tells us that it is as the Son perfected forevermore that He is appointed High Priest in the heavens.

The words open to us the inmost secret of Christian perfection. The Christian has no other perfection than the perfection of Christ. The deeper his insight into the character of his Lord, as having been made perfect by being brought into perfect union with God's will through suffering and obedience, the more clearly will he apprehend wherein that redemption which Christ came to bring really consists and what is the path to its full enjoyment.

In Christ there was nothing of sinful defect or shortcoming. He was from His birth the perfect One. And yet He needed to be perfected. There was that in His human nature which needed to grow, to be strengthened and developed, and which could only thus be perfected. He had to follow on, as step by step the will of God opened up to Him, and in the midst of temptation and suffering to learn and prove what it was at any cost to do that will alone.

It is *this* Christ who is our Leader and Fore-runner, our High Priest and Redeemer. And it is as this perfection of His, this being made perfect through obedience to God's will, is revealed to us that we shall know fully what the redemption is He brings.

We learn to take Him as our example. Like Him we say, "I am come, not to do my own will, but the will of him that sent me." We accept the will of God as the one thing we have to live for and to live in. In every circumstance and trial we see and bow to the will of God. We meet every providential appointment, in every ordinary duty of daily life, as God's will. We pray to be filled with the knowledge of His will that we may enter into it in its fullness that we may stand complete in all the will of God. Whether we suffer or obey God's will, we seek to be perfected as the Master was.

We take Christ not only as our example and law in the path of perfection, but as the promise and pledge of what we are to be. All that Christ was and did as substitute, representative, head and Saviour is for us. All He does is in the power of the endless life. This perfection of His is the perfection of His life, His way of living; this life of His, perfected in obedience, is now ours. He gives us His own Spirit to breathe, to work it in us. He is the Vine; we are the branches; the very mind and disposition that was in Him on earth is communicated to us.

Yea, more; it is not only Christ in heaven who imparts to us somewhat of His Spirit, Christ himself comes to dwell in our hearts, the Christ who was made perfect through learning obedience. It is in this character that He reigns in heaven: "He became obedient unto death; therefore God highly exalted him." *It is in this character that He dwells and rules in the heart.*

The real character, the essential attribute of the life Christ lived on earth, and which He maintains in us, is this: a will perfect with God and ready at any cost to be perfected in all His will. It is this character He imparts to His own: the perfection with which He was perfected in learning obedience.

As those who are perfect in Christ, who are perfect of heart toward God, and are pressing on to be made perfect, let us live in the will of God, our one desire to be even as He was, to do God's will, to stand perfect in all the will of God.

CHAPTER TWENTY

BE PERFECT!

Let Us Press on to Perfection

"But solid food is for the fullgrown men [perfect], even those who by reason of use have their senses exercised to discern good and evil. Wherefore, leaving the doctrine of the first principles of Christ, let us press on unto perfection" (Heb. 5:14; 6:1).

THE WRITER HAD REPROVED the Hebrews for being dull of hearing; for having made no progress in the Christian life; for still being as little children who needed milk. They could not bear solid food, the deeper and more spiritual teaching in regard to the heavenly state of life into which Christ had entered, and into which He gives admission to those who are ready for it. Such our writer calls the perfect, mature or full-grown men of the house of God.

We must not connect the idea of mature or full grown with time. In the Christian life it is

not as in nature: a believer of three years old
may be counted among the mature or perfect,
while one of twenty years' standing may be but
a babe, unskilled in the word of righteousness.
Nor must we connect it with power of intellect
or maturity of judgment. These may be found
without that insight into spiritual truth, and
that longing after the highest attainable perfection in character and fellowship with God, of
which the writer is speaking.

We are told what the distinguishing charac-
teristic of the perfect is: "even those who by
reason of use have their senses exercised to discern good and evil." It is the desire after holiness, the tender conscience that longs above
everything to discern good and evil, the heart
that seeks only and always and fully to know
and do the will of God that marks the perfect.
The man who has set his heart upon being holy,
and in the pursuit after the highest moral and
spiritual perfection exercises his senses in everything to discern good and evil, is counted the
perfect man.

The Epistle has spoken of the two stages of
the Christian life. It now calls upon the Hebrews
to be no longer babes, no longer to remain content with the first principles, the mere elements
of the doctrine of Christ. With the exhortation
"Let us press on to perfection," it invites them

to come and learn how Jesus is a Priest in the power of an endless life who can save completely; how He is the meditator of a better covenant, lifting us into a better life by writing the law in our heart; how the Holiest of all has been set open for us to enter in, and there to serve the living God.

"Let us go on to perfection" is the waymark pointing all to that heavenly life in God's presence which can be lived even here on earth, to which the full knowledge of Jesus as our heavenly High Priest leads us.[6]

"Let us press on to perfection." It is not the first time we have the word in the Epistle. We read of God's perfecting Christ through suffering. Perfection is that perfect union with God's will, that blessed meekness and surrender to God's will, which the Father wrought in Christ through His suffering.

We read of Christ's learning obedience, and so being made perfect. This is the true maturity or perfection, the true wisdom among the perfect, the knowing and doing God's will. We read of strong food for the perfect, who *by reason of use* have their senses exercised to discern good and evil. Here again perfection is, even as with Christ, the disposition, the character that is formed when a man makes conformity to God's will, fellowship with God in His holiness, the one aim of His life to which everything else, even life itself, is to be sacrificed.

It is to this that Jesus our High Priest and the further teaching of the Epistle would lead us on. The knowledge of the mysteries of God, of the highest spiritual truth, cannot profit us. We have no inward capacity for receiving them, except as our inmost life is given up to receive the perfection with which Jesus was perfected as ours.

When this disposition is found, the Holy Spirit will reveal to us how Christ hath perfected forever, in the power of an endless life, those who are sanctified. He has prepared a life, a disposition, with which He clothes them. And we shall understand that "let us go on to perfection" just means this: "Let us go on to know Christ perfectly, to live entirely by His heavenly life now He is perfected, to follow wholly His earthly life and the path in which He reached perfection."

Union with Christ in heaven will mean likeness to Christ on earth in that lamblike meekness and humility in which He suffered, in that Sonlike obedience through which He entered the glory. Brethren, leaving the doctrine of the first principles, let us go on to perfection.

CHAPTER TWENTY-ONE

BE PERFECT!

No Perfection by the Law

"Now if there was perfection through the Levitical priesthood (for under it hath the people received the law), what further need that another priest should arise after the order of Melchisedek? ... Who hath been made, not after the law of a carnal commandment, but after the power of an endless life. ... For there is a disannuling of a foregoing commandment because of its weakness and unprofitableness (for the law made nothing perfect)" (Heb. 7: 11–19).

"Gifts and sacrifices are offered, which cannot, as touching the conscience, make the worshipper perfect" (Heb. 9: 9).

"For the law having a shadow of the good things to come, ... can never ... make perfect them that draw nigh" (Heb. 10: 1).

"That apart from us they should not be made perfect" (Heb. 11: 40).

O F THE EPISTLES of the New Testament there is none in which the word *perfect* is used so often as that to the Hebrews. There is none that will help us more to see what Christian perfection is, and the way to its attainment. The word is used thrice of our Lord Jesus, and His being made perfect himself. Twice of our subjective perfection. Five times of the perfection of which the law was the shadow but which could not be till Jesus came. Thrice of Christ's work in perfecting us. And once of the work of God in perfecting us. These five thoughts will each give us a subject of meditation. Of the first two we have spoken already.

A careful perusal of the verses placed above will show that the writer thought it of great importance to make it clear that the law could perfect no person or thing. It was all the more of consequence to press this, both because of the close connection in which the law stood to the true perfection, as its promise and preparation, and of the natural tendency of the human heart to seek perfection by the law.

It was not only the Hebrews who greatly needed this teaching. Among Christians in our days the greatest hindrance in accepting the perfection the gospel asks and offers is that they make the law its standard, and then our impotence to fulfill the law, the excuse for not attaining, for not even seeking it. They have never understood that the law is but a preparation for something better; and that when that which is perfect is come, that which is in part is done away.[7]

The law demands; the law calls to effort; the law means self. It puts self upon doing its utmost. But it makes nothing perfect, neither the conscience nor the worshipper. This is what Christ came to bring. The very perfection which the law could not give He does give. The Epistle tells us that He was made a Priest, not as Aaron, after the law and in connection with the service of a carnal commandment which had to be disannulled because of its weakness and unprofitableness, but after the power of an endless life.

What Christ, as Priest, has wrought and now works, is all in the power of an inward birth, of a new life, of the eternal life. What is born into me, what is as a spirit and life within me, has its own power of growth and action. Christ's being made perfect himself through suffering and obedience; His having perfected us by that sacrifice by which He was perfected himself; and His communication of that perfection to us, is all in the power of an endless life. It works in us as a life power; in no other way could we become partakers of it.

Perfection is not through the law; let us listen to the blessed lesson. Let us take the warning. The law is so closely connected with perfection, was so long its only representative and fore-runner, that we can hardly realize that the law makes nothing perfect. Let us take the encouragement: What the law could not do (10:1), God, sending His Son, hath done.

The Son, perfected forevermore, hath perfected us forever. It is in Jesus we have our perfection. It is in living union with Him; it is when He is within us, not only as a seed or a little child but formed within us, dwelling within us, that we shall know how far He can make us perfect. It is faith that leads us in the path of perfection. It is the faith that sees, that receives, that lives in Jesus the perfect One, that will bear us on to the perfection God would have.

CHAPTER TWENTY-TWO

BE PERFECT!

Christ Hath Perfected Us

"But Christ, . . . through the greater and more perfect tabernacle, . . . through his own blood, entered in once for all into the holy place" (Heb. 9:11, 12).

"By one offering he hath perfected for ever them that are sanctified" (Heb. 10:14).

IN CHRIST'S WORK, as set before us in the Epistle to the Hebrews, there are two parts. In contrast with the worldly sanctuary, He is the minister of the true tabernacle. The Holiest of all is now open to us: Christ has opened the way through *a more perfect tabernacle* into the presence of God. He has prepared and opened up for us a place of perfect fellowship with God, of access, in a life of faith, which means a life in full union with Christ, into God's immediate presence.

There must be harmony between the place of worship and the worshipper. As He has prepared the perfect sanctuary, the Holiest of all, for us, He has prepared us for it too. "By one offering he hath perfected for ever them that are sanctified"—for the sanctuary, the sanctified ones; for the Holiest of all, a holy priesthood; for the perfect tabernacle, the perfected worshipper.

"By one offering He hath perfected for ever them that are sanctified." The word perfected cannot mean here anything different from what it meant in the three passages where it has been previously used of Him (2:11; 5:9; 7:28). They all point to that which constituted the real value, the innermost nature, of His sacrifice. He was himself perfected for our sakes, that He might perfect us with the same perfection with which God had perfected Him.

What is this perfection with which God perfected Him through suffering, in which He was perfected through obedience, in which as the Son, perfected forevermore, He was made our High Priest?

The answer is to be found in what the object was of Christ's redeeming work. The perfection of man as created consisted in this: he had a will with power to will as God willed, and so to enter into inner union with the divine

life and holiness and glory. His fall was a turn-
ing from the will of God to do the will of self.
And so this self and self-will became the source
and the curse of sin.

The work of Christ was to bring man back
to that will of God in which alone is life and
blessedness. Therefore it became God, it was
proper and needful if He was to be the Leader
of our salvation, that God should make Him
perfect through suffering. In His own person He
was to conquer sin, to develop and bring to perfection a real human life, sacrificing everything
that men hold dear, willing to give up even life
itself, in surrender to God's will; proving that
it is the meat, the very life of man's spirit, to do
God's will.

This was the perfection with which Christ
was perfected as our High Priest, who brings us
back to God. This was the meaning and the value
of His sacrifice, that "one sacrifice" by which
"he hath perfected for ever them that are sanctified." In the same sacrifice in which He was
perfected He perfected us. As the second Adam
He made us partakers of His own perfection.
Just as Adam in his death corrupted us and our
nature forevermore, so Christ, in His death, in
which He himself was perfected, perfected us
and our nature forevermore. He hath wrought out
for us a new perfect nature, a new life. With

Him we died unto sin; in Him we live unto God.

And how do we become partakers of this perfection with which Christ hath perfected us? First of all, the conscience is perfected so that we have no more conscience of sin, and enter boldly into the Holiest, the presence of God. The consciousness of a perfect redemption possesses and fills the soul.

And then, as we abide in this, God himself perfects us in every good thing to do His will, working in us that which is pleasing in His sight, *through Jesus Christ*. Through Christ, the High Priest in the power of the endless life, there comes to us in a constant stream from on high the power of the heavenly life. So that day by day we may present ourselves perfect in Christ Jesus.

A soul that seeks to dwell in the divine perfection of which the Epistle speaks; that holds fellowship with Him who in such intense human reality was perfected through suffering and obedience; that in faith turns to Him who has perfected us, and now holds our perfection in himself to be communicated as a life in us day by day, for us to practice and put it into exercise in walking in His footsteps; may count most surely that He himself will lead it into the promised inheritance.

CHAPTER TWENTY-THREE

BE PERFECT!

God Perfect You in Every Good Thing

"Now the God of peace, who brought again from the dead the great shepherd of the sheep, with the blood of an eternal covenant, even our Lord Jesus, make you perfect in every good thing to do his will, working in us that which is well-pleasing in his sight, through Jesus Christ; to whom be the glory for ever and ever. Amen" (Heb. 13:20, 21).

THESE TWO VERSES contain a summary of the whole Epistle in the form of a prayer. In the former of the two we have the substance of what was taught in the first or doctrinal half—what God *has done* for us in the redemption in Christ Jesus. In the second of the two verses we have a revelation and a promise of what this God of redemption *will do* for us. We see how God's one aim and desire is *to make us perfect*.

We have said before, the word *perfect* here implies the removal of all that is wrong and the supply of all that is wanting.[5] This is what God waits to do in us. God *"make you perfect in every good thing."*

We need a large faith to claim this promise. That our faith may be full and strong, we are reminded of what God has done for us; this is the assurance of what He will yet do in us.

Let us look to Him as *the God of peace,* who has made peace in the entire putting away of sin; who now proclaims peace; who gives perfect peace. Let us look to *Jesus Christ, the Great Shepherd of the sheep,* our High Priest and King, who loves to care for and keep us. Let us remember *the blood of an eternal covenant,* in the power of which God raised Him and He entered heaven; that blood is God's pledge that that covenant with its promises will be fulfilled in our hearts. Let us think of God's *bringing Him again from the dead,* that our faith and hope might be in God: the power that raised Jesus is the power that works in us.

Yes, let us look and worship and adore this God of peace, who has done it all, who raised Christ through the blood of the covenant, that we might know and trust Him.

And let us believe the message that tells us:

This God of peace will perfect us in every good thing. The God who *perfected Christ* will *perfect us too.* The God who worked out such a perfect salvation *for us,* will perfect it *in us.* The more we gaze upon Him who has done such wondrous things for us, the more will we trust Him for this wondrous thing He promises to do in us—to perfect us in every good thing.

What God did in Christ is the measure of what He will do in us to make us perfect. The same Omnipotence that wrought in Christ to perfect Him waits for our faith to trust its working in us day by day to perfect us in the doing of God's will. And on our part, the surrender to be made perfect will be the measure of our capacity to apprehend what God has done in Christ.

And now hear what this perfection is which this God promises to work in us. It is truly divine, as divine as the work of redemption: *the God of peace,* who brought again Christ from the dead, *perfect you.* It is intensely practical: in every *good thing* to do His will. It is universal, with nothing excluded from its operation: in *every* good thing. It is truly human and personal: God perfects us so that *we do His will.* It is inward: God working *in us* that which is pleasing in His sight. And it is most blessed, giving us the consciousness that our life pleases

Him, because it is His own work: He works in
us *that which is pleasing in His sight.*

God "perfect you to do his will"—this is
the conclusion of the whole Epistle. "To do his
will"—this is the blessedness of the angels in
heaven. For this the Son became man; by this
He was perfected; in this—"in the which will,"
as done by Him—"we are sanctified." It is *"to
do his will"* that God perfects us; that God works
in us that which is pleasing in His sight.

Believer, let God's aim be yours. Say to God
that you do desire this above everything else.
Give yourself, at once, entirely, absolutely, to
this, and say with the Son, "Lo, I come to do thy
will, O my God." This will give you an insight
into the meaning and the need and the preciousness of the promise, God "perfect you to do his
will." This will fix your heart upon God in the
wondrous light of the truth: He who perfected
Christ is perfecting me too. This will give you
confidence, in the fullness of faith, to claim this
God as your God, the God who perfects in every
good thing.

The perfecting of the believer by God, restoring him to his right condition to fit him for doing His will, may be instantaneous. A valuable
piece of machinery may be out of order. The
owner has spent time and trouble in vain to put
it right. The maker comes; it takes him but a

moment to see and remove the hindrance. And so the soul that has for years wearied itself in the effort to do God's will may often in one moment be delivered from some misapprehension as to what God demands or promises, and find itself restored, perfected for every good thing. And what was done in a moment becomes the secret of the continuous life, as faith each day claims the God that perfects to do that which is well-pleasing in His sight.

Yes, the soul that dares say to God that it yields itself in everything to do His will, and through all the humiliation which comes from the sense of emptiness and impotence abides by its vow in simple trust, will be made strong to rise and to appropriate and experience in full measure what God has offered in this precious word: The God of peace perfect you in every good thing to do His will, working in you that which is pleasing in His sight, through Jesus Christ.

And it will sing with new meaning and in fullness of joy the song of adoring love: To Him be glory forever and ever. Amen.

CHAPTER TWENTY-FOUR

BE PERFECT!

Perfect Patience Makes a Perfect Man

"And let patience have its perfect work, that ye may be perfect and entire, lacking in nothing" (Jas. 1:4).

PERFECTION IS A SEED. The life given in regeneration is a perfect life. Through ignorance and unbelief the soul may never get beyond knowing that it has life, and remain unconscious of what a wonderful perfect life it has.

Perfection is a seed. It is a blessed hour when the soul awakens to know this and with a perfect heart yields itself to appropriate all that God has given. The perfection of the perfect heart, a heart wholly yielded to seek God with all its strength, is again a seed with infinite power of growth and increase.

Perfection is a growth. As the Christian awakens to the consciousness of what God asks and gives, and maintains the vow of a whole-hearted surrender, he grows in his sense of need and his trust in the promise of a divine life and strength until all the promises of grace come to a focus in the one assurance, "The God of all grace shall himself perfect you"; that faith which was the fruit of previous growth becomes the new seed of further growth.

Perfection now develops into something riper and mellower. The overshadowing presence of Him who perfects rests abidingly on the spirit, and the whole character bears the impress of heavenliness and fellowship with the Unseen. The soul makes way for God and gives Him time to do His work. The God of peace, perfecting in every good thing, gets entire possession. The soul rests in the rest of God.

This is not the work of a day. Perfection is a growth. "Ye have need *of patience,* that, having done the will of God, ye may receive the promise." "Be imitators of them who through faith and patience inherit the promises." Man is the creature of time, is under the law of development.

In the kingdom of heaven it is as in nature— from the seed first the blade, then the ear, then the full corn in the ear. There is nothing at times that appears more mysterious to the believer than the slowness of God. It is as if our prayers are not heard, as if His promises are not fulfilled, as if our faith is vain. And all the time God is hastening on His work with all speed. He will avenge His own elect speedily, though He bear long with them.

"Let patience have its *perfect* work." We are so often impatient with ourselves, not content to trust God to do His work, and so hindering just when we want to hurry on His work. We are impatient with God. Instead of the adoring trust of Him, the God of peace, who is perfecting us, we fret ourselves because we see not what we had thought out for ourselves.

"Rest in the Lord, and wait patiently for him" is the law of faith, not only in times of weal, but specially in the path of perfection. Faith is the law of the Christian life to an extent that very few realize. The assurance that rests in the unseen power that is working out its holy purpose will never be disappointed. As it has been said of an aged saint, "She was sure that, however long any soul might have to continue in the path of humiliation, with self-emptying, the end, with all who were faithful, would one day be a filling to overflowing of all their inward being with the presence of the Holy One."

"Let patience have its perfect work." This

is the command. To those who obey it the prospect held out is sure: "that *ye* may be *perfect
and entire,* lacking in nothing." How words are
heaped up to make us feel what the aim and expectation of the believer ought to be! *Perfect,*
something finished, that answers its end; *entire,*
that in which every part is in its place; and
lacking in nothing, just all that the Father expects: such is the Christian character as God's
Spirit sets it before us.

There is a perfection which the Christian is
to regard as his duty and his life. Where patience
has its perfect work it will bring forth what the
husbandman longs for—fruit unto perfection.
God's work in man is *the man.* If God's teaching by patience have a perfect work in you, you
are perfect.

But where there is to be this perfect fruit,
there must first be the perfect seed. And that
seed is the perfect heart. Without this, whence
could patience have its perfect work? With this,
every trial, every difficulty, every failure even,
is accepted as God's training school, and God
is trusted as the Faithful One, who is perfecting His own work. Let there be first the perfect
heart—that will lead to perfect patience, and that
again to the fully perfected man.

Jesus Christ was himself not perfected in
one day: it took time; in Him patience had its

perfect work. True faith recognizes the need of time, and rests in God.

Time to us means days and years. Let us learn each day to renew the vow: This day I would live for God as perfectly as His grace will enable me. This day I would, in the patience of hope, trust the God of all grace, who himself is perfecting me. This day I would be perfect and entire, lacking nothing. With such a vow renewed day by day, with faith in Christ who has perfected us, and God who is perfecting us, patience will do its perfect work. And we shall be perfect and entire, lacking nothing.

CHAPTER TWENTY-FIVE

BE PERFECT!

The Perfect Tongue
Marks the Perfect Man

"In many things we all stumble. If any stumbleth not in word, the same is a perfect man, able to bridle the whole body also" (Jas. 3:2).

THERE CAN BE no perfection in art or science without attention to little things. One of the truest marks of genius is the power, in presence of the highest ideal, to attend to even the least details. No chain is stronger than its feeblest link. The weakest point in the character of a Christian is the measure of his nearness to perfection. It is in the little things of daily life that perfection is attained and proved.

The tongue is a little member. A word of the tongue is oh such a little thing in the eyes of many. And yet we are told by none less than our blessed Lord: "By thy words shalt thou be justified." When the Son of man shall come in the glory of His Father to render to every man according to his deeds, every word will be taken into account.

In the light of the great day of God, if any man stumble not in word, the same is a perfect man. This is the full-grown man, who has attained maturity, who has reached unto the measure of the stature of the fullness of Christ.

But is it possible for any man to be thus perfect and not to stumble in a single word? Has not James just said, "In many things we all stumble"? Just think of all the foolish words one hears among Christians: the sharp words, the hasty, thoughtless, unloving words, the words that are only half honest and not spoken from the heart. Think of all the sins of the tongue against the law of perfect love and perfect truth, and we must admit the terrible force of James' statement: "In many things we all stumble." When he adds, "If any stumbleth not in word, the same is a perfect man," can he really mean that God expects that we should live so, and that we must seek and expect it too?

Let us think. With what object does he use these words? In the beginning of his Epistle he had spoken of patience having its perfect work, that we may be perfect and entire, lacking in nothing. There, entire perfection, with nothing lacking, is set before us as a definite promise to those who let patience have its perfect work. His Epistle is written, as all the Epistles are, under the painful impression of how far ordinary Christian experience is from such perfection, but in the faith that it is no hopeless task to teach God's people that they ought to be, that they can be, perfect and entire, lacking in nothing.

Where he begins to speak of the tongue, the two sides of the truth again rise up before him. The ordinary experience he expresses in the general statement: "In many things we all stumble." The will of God and the power of grace he sets forth in the blessed and not impossible ideal of all who seek to be perfect and entire: "If any man stumble not in word, the same is a perfect man." James speaks of it in all simplicity as a condition as actual as the other of all stumbling.

The question is again asked: But is it really a possible ideal? Does God expect it of us? Is grace promised for it? Let us call in Peter as a witness and listen to what God's Spirit says through him as to that terrible necessity of always stumbling which some hold fast, as to the blessed possibility of being kept from stumbling. "Give the more diligence," he writes, "to make your calling and election sure; for if ye do these

things, *ye shall never stumble.*" "Never," that
includes not even in word. Let us hear what
Jude says, "Now unto him, who is able to *guard
you from stumbling* through Jesus Christ our
Lord, be glory, majesty, dominion, and power,
before all time, . . . and now, and for evermore.
Amen." It is the soul that knows and without
ceasing trusts God as a *God who guards from
stumbling,* as a God who watches and keeps us
every moment through Jesus Christ, that will
without ceasing sing this song of praise.

The three texts on stumbling are the only
ones in the New Testament in which the word
occurs in reference to the Christian life. That
in James one hears quoted a hundred times for
once that those in Peter and Jude are cited.

Christ has said, "According to your faith be
it unto you." If our faith feeds only and always
on, "In many things we all stumble," no wonder
that we do stumble. If with that *stumble* we
take the *stumble not* that follows, "If any man
stumble not in word, the same is a perfect man,"
and the "not stumble" of Peter and Jude, the
faith that embraces the promise will obtain it.
God's power will translate it into our experience,
and our life will be a living Epistle into which
God's words have been transcribed.

Out of the abundance of the heart the mouth
speaketh. Out of a heart that is perfect towards

God, in which the love of God is shed abroad, in which Christ dwelleth, the tongue will bring forth words of truth and uprightness, of love and gentleness, full of beauty and of blessing. God wills it. God works it. Let us claim it.

CHAPTER TWENTY-SIX

BE PERFECT!

God Shall Himself Perfect You

"The God of all grace, who called you unto his eternal glory in Christ, after that ye have suffered a little while, shall himself perfect, stablish, strengthen you. To him be the dominion for ever and ever. Amen" (I Pet. 5: 10, 11).

THROUGH SUFFERING TO GLORY: this is the keynote of the First Epistle of Peter. The word suffer occurs sixteen times, the word glory fourteen times. In its closing words the readers are reminded of all its teaching, as he writes to them: "The God of all grace, who called you unto his eternal *glory*, after that ye have *suffered* a little while."

In no Epistle of the New Testament are the two aspects of Christ's death—that He suffered for us and that we are to suffer with Him and like Him—so clearly and closely linked together. Fellowship with Christ, likeness to Christ, manifested in suffering, is the point of view from which Peter would have us look on life as the path to glory. To be a partaker of the sufferings and the glory of Christ is the Christian's privilege. He was perfected through suffering by God: the same God perfects us for suffering and glorifying Him in it.

"God . . . shall himself perfect . . . you!" In God alone is perfection. In Him is all perfection. And all perfection comes from Him. When we consider the wondrous perfection there is in the sun, in the laws it obeys, and in the blessings it dispenses, and remember that it owes all to the will of the Creator, we acknowledge that its perfection is from God. And so, through the whole of nature, to the tiniest insect that floats in the sunbeam and the humblest little flower that basks in its light, everything owes its beauty to God alone. All His works praise Him. His work is perfect.

And have we not here in nature the open secret of Christian perfection? It is God who must perfect us! "God . . . shall himself perfect . . . you." What is revealed in nature is the pledge of what is secured to us in grace. "It became him, for whom are all things, and of whom are all things, in leading many sons unto glory, to make the author [Leader] of their salvation perfect through suffering." It was the beseeming thing that God should show that He is the God who works out perfection amid the weakness and suffering of a human life. This is what constitutes the very essence of salvation, to be perfected of God, to yield oneself to the God, for whom and of whom are all things, Himself to perfect us.

God hath planted deep in the heart of man the desire after perfection. Is it not this that stirs the spirit of the artist and the poet, of the discoverer and the artificer? Is it not the nearest possible approach to this that wakens admiration and enthusiasm? And is it only in grace that all thought and all joy of present perfection is to be banished? Certainly not, if God's Word be true.

The promise is sure and bright for this our earthly life: "God . . . shall himself perfect . . . you." The "himself perfect you" can refer to nothing but the present daily life. God shall himself put you into the right position, and in that position then stablish and strengthen you, so as to fit you perfectly for the life you have to live and the work you have to do.

We find it so hard to believe this, because we do not know what it means. "Ye are not under the law, but under grace." The law demands what we cannot give or do. Grace never asks what it does not give; and so the Father never asks what we cannot do. He himself who raised Jesus from the dead is always ready, in that same resurrection power, to perfect us to do His will. Let us believe and be still until our soul is filled with the blessed truth, and we know that it will be done to us.

O my soul, learn to know this God and claim Him, in this His character, as thine: "God . . . shall himself perfect . . . you!" Worship and adore Him here until thy faith is filled with the assurance: my God himself is perfecting me. Regard thyself as clay in the hands of the Great Artist, spending all His thought and time and love to make thee perfect. Yield thyself in voluntary, loving obedience to His will and His Spirit. Yield thyself in full confidence into His very hands, and let the words ring through thy whole being: *God shall himself perfect thee,* perfectly fit thee for all He would have thee be or do. Let every perfect bud or flower thou meetest whisper its message: only let God work; only wait thou upon God; God shall himself perfect thee.

Believer, hast thou longed for this? O claim it, claim it now. Or rather, claim now in very deed this God as thy God. Just as the writer to the Hebrews, and Peter in this Epistle, gather up all their varied teaching into this one central promise, "God . . . shall himself perfect . . . you," so there may come in the life of the believer a moment when he gathers up all his desires and efforts, all his knowledge of God's truth, and all his faith in God's promises, concentrates them in one simple act of surrender and trust, and, yielding himself wholly to do His will, dares to claim God as the God that perfects him. And his life becomes one doxology of adoring love: To Him be the dominion for ever and ever. Amen.

CHAPTER TWENTY-SEVEN

BE PERFECT!

Perfect Love:
Keeping Christ's Word

"Whoso keepeth his word, in him verily hath the love of God been perfected" (I John 2:5).

TAULER SAYS of the Apostle John: "In three ways, dear children, did the beloved Lord attract to himself the heart of John.

"First, the Lord Jesus called him out of the world to make him an apostle.

"Next, He granted to him to rest upon His loving breast.

"Third, and this was the greatest and most perfect nearness, when on the holy day of Pentecost He gave to him the Holy Ghost, and opened to him the door through which he should pass into the heavenly places.

"Thus, children, does the Lord first call you

from the world and make you to be the messengers of God. Next, He draws you close to
himself that you may learn to know His holy
gentleness and lowliness, His deep and burning
love, and His perfect unshrinking obedience.

"And yet this is not all. Many have been
drawn thus far and are satisfied to go no further. And yet they are far from the perfect nearness which the heart of Jesus desires.

"St. John lay at one moment on the breast
of the Lord Jesus, and then He forsook Him and
fled.

"If you have been brought so far as to rest
on the breast of Christ, it is well. But yet there
was to John a nearness still to come, one moment
of which would be worth a hundred years of all
that had gone before. The Holy Ghost was given
to him—the door was opened.

"There is a nearness in which we lose ourselves, and God is all in all. This may come to us
in one swift moment, or we may wait for it with
longing hearts, and learn to know it at last. It
was of this St. Paul spoke when he said that the
thing which the heart hath not conceived, God
hath now revealed to us by His Holy Spirit. The
soul is drawn within the inner chamber, and
there are the wonders and the riches revealed."[8]

To understand a writer it is often needful

to know his character and history. When John wrote the Epistle, he had for fifty years been living in that inmost nearness of which Tauler speaks, in the inner chamber within the veil. While on earth Jesus had found in him a congenial spirit, receptive of His highest spiritual teaching, one to whom He felt drawn in special love. Fifty years of communion with the Son in the glory of the Father, and experience of the power of the Holy Spirit to make the eternal life, the heavenly life of Jesus in fellowship with the Father, an everyday reality!

No wonder that when John testifies of it as a life of perfect love, the Church that is not living on this level can only speak of it as an ideal, in this life unattainable. To one who thinks of what John was and knew of his Lord, and what a Church under his teaching would be, the words are simply descriptive of characters he saw around him; men to whom he could write: "Beloved, if our hearts condemn us not, we have boldness toward God . . . because we keep his commandments, and do the things that are pleasing in his sight." "Whoso keepeth his word, in him verily hath the love of God been perfected."[9]

John is the disciple whom Jesus loved! When Jesus spoke about the love of God, the words had a special attraction for him; the love with which Jesus loved him exercised its mighty influence; the Holy Spirit that came from the heart of the glorified Jesus intensified and spiritualized it all; and John became the Apostle of Love, who, gazing into the very depths of the divine glory and being, found there that God is love.

With this word love as the sum of his theology, he links the word he found in the Old Testament and in the writings of his brother apostles, the word *perfect*, and tells us that this is perfection, this the highest type of Christian character, the highest attainment of the Christian life—for a man to have God's love perfected in him.

The condition and the mark of this being perfected in love Jesus had taught him: "If a man love me, he will keep my word: and my Father will love him; and we will come unto him, and make our abode with him."

Keeping His Word: this is the link between the love of the disciple and the love of the Father, leading to that wondrous union in which the Father's love draws Him to come and dwell in the loving heart. "If ye keep my commandments," Jesus said, "ye shall abide in my love: even as I have kept my Father's commandments, and abide in his love." And John confirms from his own experience what the Master spake:

"Whoso keepeth his word, in him verily hath the love of God been perfected."

Thank God! this is a life to be found on earth. God's love can be perfected in us. Let not what we see in the Church around us make us doubt God's Word. When John spoke of perfect love, and Paul of the love of God shed abroad in our hearts by the Holy Ghost, they testified from personal experience of what they had received in direct communication from the throne of glory. The words were to them the expression of a life of which we have little conception; to us they convey no more truth than our low experience can put into them.

Oh! that our hearts might be roused to believe in their heavenly, supernatural, fullness of meaning, and not to rest until we know that the love that passeth knowledge, the love that God is, the love of Christ, dwells within us as a fountain springing up unto everlasting life. *"The love of God perfected in us"*—the prospect is sure to everyone who will allow the love of God in Christ to have the mastery, and to prove what God can do for them that love Him.

CHAPTER TWENTY-EIGHT

BE PERFECT!

Perfect Love:
Loving the Brethren

"Beloved, if God so loved us, we also ought to love one another. No man hath beheld God at any time: if we love one another, God abideth in us, and his love is perfected in us" (I John 4: 11, 12).

THE FIRST MARK of a soul in whom the love of God is to be perfected is *keeping His Word.* The path of obedience, the loving obedience of the perfect heart, the obedience of a life wholly given up to God's will, is the path the Son opened up into the presence and the love of the Father. It is the only path that leads into perfect love.

The commandments of Christ are all included in the one word love, because "love is the fulfilling of the law." "A new commandment I

have given you, that ye love one another, even
as I have loved you." This is Christ's word: he
that keeps this word, keeps all the commandments. Love to the brethren is the second mark
of a soul seeking to enter the life of perfect love.

In the very nature of things it cannot be
otherwise. "Love seeketh not her own": love
loses itself in going out to live in others. Love
is the death of self: where self still lives there
can be no thought of perfect love. Love is the
very being and glory of God; it is His nature and
property as God to give of His own life to all
His creatures, to communicate His own goodness and blessedness. The gift of His Son is the
gift of himself to be the life and joy of man.
When that love of God enters the heart, it imparts its own nature—the desire to give itself
to the very death for others. When the heart
wholly yields itself to be transformed into this
nature and likeness, then love takes possession;
there the love of God is perfected.

The question is often asked whether it be
the love of God to us, or our love to God, that
is meant by perfect love. The word includes
both, because it implies a great deal more. The
love of God is One, as God is One: His life, His
very being. Where that love descends and enters, it retains its nature; it is ever the divine
life and love within us. God's love to us, and

our love to God and Christ, our love to the brethren and to all men—all these are but aspects of one and the same love. Just as there is one Holy Spirit in God and in us, so it is one divine love, the love of the Spirit, that dwells in God and in us.

To know this is a wonderful help to faith. It teaches us that to love God, or the brethren, or our enemies, is not a thing our efforts can attain. We can do it only because the divine love is dwelling in us; only as far as we yield ourselves to the divine love as a living power within, as a life that has been born into us, and that the Holy Spirit strengthens into action. Our part is first of all to rest, to cease from effort, to know that He is in us, and to give way to the love that dwells and works in us in a power that is from above.

How well John remembered the night when Jesus spoke so wonderfully of love in His parting words! How impossible it appeared to the disciples indeed to love as He had loved! How much there had been among them of pride, and envy, and selfishness—anything but love like His! How it had broken out among them that very night at the supper table! They never could love like the Master—it was impossible.

But what a change was wrought when the risen One breathed on them and said, "Receive

ye the Holy Ghost!'' And how that change was
consummated when the Holy Spirit came down
from heaven, and out of that wonderful love
which flowed in holy interchange between
the Father and the Son when they met again in
the glory, shed abroad in their hearts *the love
of God!* In the love of the day of Pentecost, the
perfect love celebrated its first great triumph in
the hearts of men.

The love of God still reigns. The Spirit of
God still waits to take possession of hearts where
He has hitherto had too scanty room. He had
been in the disciples all the time, but they had
not known of what manner of spirit they were.
He had come upon them on that evening when
the risen One breathed upon them. But it was
on Pentecost He filled them so that love divine
prevailed and overflowed and they were perfected in love.

Let every effort we make to love, and every
experience of how feeble our love is, lead us
and draw us on to Jesus on the throne. In Him
the love of God is revealed and glorified and
rendered accessible to us. Let us believe that the
love of God can come down as a fire that will
consume and destroy self, and make love to one
another, fervent perfect love, the one mark of
discipleship. Let us believe that this love of God,
perfect love, can be shed abroad in our hearts,

in measure to us hitherto unknown, by the Holy Ghost given to us. Our tongues and lives, our homes and churches, will then prove to sinful, perishing fellow men that there still are children of God in whom the love of God is perfected.

Even as the whole Christian life, so love too has its two stages. There is love seeking, struggling, and doing its best to obey, and ever failing. And there is love finding, resting, rejoicing, and ever triumphing. This takes place when self and its efforts have been given into the grave of Jesus, and *His life and love* have taken their place. The birth of heavenly love in the soul has come. In the power of the heavenly life, to love is natural and easy. Christ dwells in the heart; now we are rooted and grounded in love, and know the love that passeth knowledge.

CHAPTER TWENTY-NINE

BE PERFECT!

Perfect Love:
God Abiding in Us

"No man hath beheld God at any time: if we love one another, God abideth in us, and his love is perfected in us: hereby we know that we abide in him and he in us, because he hath given us of his Spirit" (I John 4: 12, 13).

NO MAN HATH BEHELD GOD at any time." The vision of God we may not yet have. The all-consuming, all-absorbing fire of its glory, bringing death to all that is of nature, is not consistent with this our earthly state. But there is given to us in its stead an equivalent that can prepare and train us for the beatific vision, and also satisfy the soul with all that it can contain of God.

We cannot behold God, but we can have *God abiding in us,* and *His love perfected in us.*

Though the brightness of God's glory is not now
to be seen, the presence of what is the very
essence of that glory—His love—may now be
known. God's love perfected in us, God himself
abiding in us—this is the heaven we can have
on earth.

And the way to this blessedness? God abideth in us, and His love is perfected in us, *if we
love one another.* We may not behold God; but
we behold our brother, and, lo! in him we have
an object that will repay us for the loss of the
vision of God. This object will awaken and call
forth the divine love within us; will exercise
and strengthen and develop it; will open the
way for the divine love to do its beloved work
through us, and so to perfect us in love; will
waken the divine complacency and draw it down
to come and take up its abode within us.

In my brother I have an object on which
God bids me prove all my love to him. In loving
him, however unlovely he may be, love proves
that self no longer lives; that it is a flame of
that fire which consumed the Lamb of God;
that it is God's love being perfected in us; that
it is God himself living and loving within us.

"If we love one another, God abideth in us.
. . . Hereby we know that we abide in him and he
in us, because he hath given us of his Spirit."
The wondrous knowledge that God abides in us

and His love is perfected in us is no result of reflection, a deduction from what we see in ourselves. No, divine things, divine love, the divine indwelling, are only seen in a divine light. Hereby know we them because He hath given us of His Spirit. John remembers how little the disciples understood or experienced of the words of Jesus until that never-to-be-forgotten day when, in the light of the fire that came from heaven, all became luminous and real.

It is the Holy Spirit alone, not in His ordinary gracious workings such as the disciples too had before that day, but in His special bestowment direct from the throne of the exalted Jesus who makes Him personally and permanently present to the soul that will rest content with nothing less. It is the Holy Spirit alone by whom we know that God dwelleth in us, and we in Him, and that His love is perfected in us.

It is in the Christian life now even as it was then. It is the special work of the Holy Spirit to reveal the indwelling God and to perfect us in love. By slow steps we have to master now one side of truth and then another; to practice now one grace and then the very opposite. For a time our whole heart goes out in the aim to know and do His will.

Then again, it is as if there is but one thing

to do—to love—and we feel as if in our own home, in all our contact with men, in our outlook in the Church and the world, we need but to practice love. After a time we feel how we fail, and we turn to the Word that calls us to faith, to cease from self and to trust in Him who works both to will and to do. Here once more we come short, and we feel that this alone can meet our need—a share in the Pentecostal gift—the Spirit given in power as not before. Let none faint or be discouraged. Let us seek to obey and to love and to trust with a perfect heart. In that whereunto we have attained let us be faithful. But so let us press on to perfection. Let us confidently expect that this portion too of the Word will be made all our own: "If we love one another, God abideth in us, and the love of God is perfected in us. Hereby we know [it], because he hath given us of his Spirit."

It is only in the path of love—love in practical exercise seeking to be perfect love—that this wondrous blessing can be found: God abiding in us, and we in Him. And it is only by the Holy Ghost that we can know that we have it. God abiding in us and His love perfected in us: God is love; how sure it is that He longs to abide with us!

God is love, who sends forth the Spirit of His Son to fill the hearts that are open to Him.

How sure it is that we can be perfected in love. A perfect heart can count upon being filled with a perfect love. Let nothing less than perfect love be our aim that we may have God abiding in us, and His love perfected in us. We shall know it by the Spirit which He hath given us.

CHAPTER THIRTY

BE PERFECT!

Perfect Love:
As He Is, Even So We

"Herein is love made perfect in us, that we may have boldness in the day of judgment: because as he is, even so are we in this world" (I John 4:17).

LET US LOOK back on the steps in the life of perfected love that have been set before us thus far. The divine love entering the heart manifests itself first in loving obedience to Christ. Of that obedience, love to the brethren in active exercise becomes the chief mark and manifestation.

In this obedient love and loving obedience, the principle of fellowship with God—God abiding in us—is developed and strengthened. Of this fellowship the Holy Spirit gives the evidence and abiding consciousness. Such is the path in which love is perfected. Obedience to Christ: love to the brethren; the indwelling of God in us, and ours in Him; the communication and revelation of all this by the Holy Spirit—all these are cor-related ideas. They imply and condition each other. Together they make up the blessed life of perfect love.

The perfect heart began by seeking God wholly and alone. It found Him in the perfect way, of obedient love to the Lord, ministering and loving to the brethren. So it came in Christ to the Father, and fellowship with Him. So it was prepared and opened for that special illumination of the Spirit which revealed God's indwelling: the Father came to take up His abode. What was at first but a little seed—the perfect heart—has grown up and borne fruit; the perfect heart is now a heart in which the love of God is perfected. Love has taken full possession, and reigns throughout the whole being.

Has the apostle now anything more that he can say of perfect love? Yes; two things. He tells what is its highest blessing: "Herein is love made perfect in us, *that* we may have boldness in the day of judgment." And what is its deepest ground or reason? "*Because* as he is, even so are we in this world." The former of these two thoughts we find again in the next verse. Let us here consider the latter.

"Because as he is, even so are we in this world." It is in Christ we are perfect. It is with the same perfection with which Christ was perfected himself that He made us perfect, that God now perfects us. Our place in Christ implies perfect unity of life and spirit, of disposition and character. John gathers up all the elements of perfect love he has mentioned and in view of the day of judgment and the boldness perfect love will give us combines them into this one, "Because as he is, even so are we in this world."

"As he is, even so are we." In chapter 2 he had said, "He that saith he abideth in him, ought himself also to walk *even as he* walked." Likeness to Christ in His walk of obedience on earth is the mark of perfect love.

In chapter 3 we read, "Every one that hath this hope set on him [the hope of being like Him, when we shall see Him as He is] purifieth [perfecteth] himself, even as he is pure." Likeness to Christ in His heavenly purity is the mark of perfect love.

In chapter 3 we read further, "Hereby know we love, because he laid down his life for us; and we ought to lay down our lives for the brethren." Likeness to Christ in His love to us is the mark of perfect love.

In the last night Jesus prayed, "That they may be one, even as we are one; I in them, and thou in me, that they may be made perfect in one." Likeness to Christ in His fellowship with the Father—God in us and we in Him—is the mark of perfect love. God gave Christ to save us by becoming our life, by taking us up into union with himself. God could have no higher aim, could bestow no higher blessing than that He should see Christ in us that we may have boldness in the day of judgment. Herein is love made perfect, "because as he is, even so are we in this world."

"That we may have boldness in the day of judgment," God hath committed judgment unto the Son, as the perfected Son of man. His judgment will be a spiritual one: himself will be its standard; likeness to Him the fitness to pass in and reign with Him.

Perfect love is perfect union and perfect likeness. We have boldness even in the day of judgment "because as he is, even so are we in this world." Oh ye seekers after perfection! it is in Christ it is to be found. In Him is God's love revealed. In Him and His life you enter into it and it enters into you. In Him love takes possession and transforms you into His likeness. In Him God comes to make His abode in you. In Him love is perfected. The prayer is fulfilled, "That the love wherewith thou lovest me may be in them, and I in them." The love of God is perfected in us; we are perfected in love; we have boldness in the day of judgment—because as He is, even so are we.

The love of God, as a fire from the altar before the throne, as the presence of the God of love himself living in us, makes itself felt in its heavenly power, so that the world may know that God has loved us as He loved His Son. The love that flows from God to Christ rests on us too and makes us one with Him. As He, the Son, is in heaven, even so are we in the world living in the Father and in His love.

CHAPTER THIRTY-ONE

BE PERFECT!

Perfect Love:
Casting Out Fear

"There is no fear in love: but perfect love casteth out fear, because fear hath punishment; and he that feareth is not made perfect in love" (I John 4:18).

BENGEL SAYS that in the religious life there are four steps: serving God without fear or love; with fear without love; with fear and love; with love without fear. Augustine says, "Fear prepares the way for love: where there is no fear, there is no opening for love to enter. Fear is the medicine, love the healing. Fear leads to love; when love is perfected fear is done. Perfect love casteth out fear. Herein is love perfected, that we may have boldness in the day of judgment: because as He is, even so are we in this world."

The day of judgment! What a day that will be! Many have no fear of that day because they trust that they have been justified. They imagine that the same grace which justified the ungodly will give the passage into heaven. This is not what Scripture teaches.

The reality of our having bestowed forgiveness will be tested in that day by our having bestowed forgiveness on others. Our fitness for entering the kingdom will be tested by the way in which we have served Jesus in the ministry of love to the sick and the hungry. In our justification all this had no part. In the judgment it will be the all-important element.

If we are to see Him as He is, and to be like Him, we must have purified ourselves as He is pure. It is perfect love, it is to be in this world *even as He is*, that casts out fear and gives us boldness in the day of judgment. He that feareth is not made perfect in love.

The day of judgment! What a day! What a blessed thing to have boldness in that day! To meet the burning, fiery furnace of God's holiness, to be ready to be judged by our conformity to Christ's likeness and image, and to have no fear, what blessedness! It is this that makes what Scripture reveals of perfection and of love perfected in us of such immediate and vital interest to each one of us.

We have come to the close of our meditations on what Scripture teaches of the perfection attainable in this life. We began with the perfect heart, the heart wholly set upon God, as the mark of the man whom God counts a perfect man. We saw the perfect man walking in a perfect way, "walking in all the commandments and ordinances of the Lord blameless." We found with the New Testament the standard at once infinitely raised—perfect as the Father, the child's standard; perfected as the Master, the disciple's model; perfect in all the will of God, the Christian's aim and hope. And then to meet this high demand, the word came to us: perfect in Christ, perfected by Christ, God himself perfecting us in every good thing.

And now John, the beloved disciple, has summed up all the teaching of the word with his perfect love. By keeping Christ's word, loving the brethren, abiding in God, filled with the Spirit, being even as Christ is, we can live perfected in love. With a heart that does not condemn us, we have boldness before God, because we keep His commandments and do the things that are pleasing in His sight. With God's love perfected in us we have boldness in the day of judgment.

Beloved fellow Christian! To have the love of God perfected in us, to be perfected in love, perfect love—these all are a divine possibility, a divine reality, the ripened fruit of the perfect life. We know now the tree on which this fruit grows. Its root is a heart perfect with God, walking before Him and being perfect.

Let us be perfect in our surrender to Him in obedience and trust. Let deep dependence on Him, let faith in Him, let a patient waiting, having our expectation from Him alone, be the spirit of our daily life. It is God himself who must give it. Let us count upon Him for nothing less than to be perfected in love and to have God abiding in us. This is what He longs to do for us.

The tree that grows on this root is a life in union with Christ, aiming at perfect conformity to Him. "Perfect in Christ, perfected by Christ, perfected by God like Christ and through Christ." When these words, pregnant with the will and love of God and the mystery of redemption, become the daily life of the soul, the perfect heart rules the life, and the believer learns to stand perfect in all the will of God, the tree brings forth fruit abundantly.

Even unto perfection. Obedience and brotherly love, fellowship with God and likeness to Christ, and the unhindered flow and rule of the Holy Spirit, lead the soul into a life of perfect love. The God of love gets His heart's desire;

the love of God celebrates its triumph; the days of heaven are begun on earth; the soul is perfected in love.

"Finally, brethren, farewell! Be perfected." *Be perfect with God.* Let nothing less be your aim. *God will show himself perfect with you,* will perfectly reveal himself, will perfectly possess you. Believe this. *God shall himself perfect you* day by day. With each new morning you may claim it. Live in the surrender to this His work, and accept it. Fear not, nor be discouraged. God himself will grant you to know what it is: God dwelleth in us, and His love is perfected in us.

A Prayer

O my Father! I would walk before Thee this day, and be perfect. Thou hast commanded it; Thou givest the enabling grace. I would be perfect with the Lord my God. I would serve Thee with a perfect heart. I would be perfect as the Father is perfect.

These are Thine own words, O my God! I would accept and obey them in childlike simplicity and trust.

I thank Thee for the unspeakable gift, Thy beloved Son, who was himself perfected through suffering and obedience in His sacrifice on the cross, and by that sacrifice hath perfected us too. I thank Thee that through Him Thou dost now perfect me in every good thing, thyself working in me that which is pleasing in Thy sight. Thou wilt show thyself strong to them that are of a perfect heart.

I thank Thee, O my Father, for the blessed prospect Thy Word holds out of being perfected in love here on earth; for the blessed witness of the beloved disciple to its truth in him and around him; for the power and light of the Holy Spirit that sheds abroad Thy love in our hearts, and makes it all a reality and a consciousness. The Lord will perfect that which concerneth me: to Him be the glory. Amen.

Notes

[1] In Hebrew there are two words translated "perfect." The one, *tam*, from a root meaning to end, to finish off, to complete. It is used of the finishing of a house, of the completion of time (a whole year). Of the sacrifices it is more than forty times used and translated *without blemish*. Used of man, it expresses the integrity or wholeness of the heart in its devotion to God. See Gen. 6:9; 17:1; Job 1:1, 8; Deut. 18:13; Ps. 101:2, 6. Also of God: Deut. 32:4; Job 37:16; Ps. 18:30, 32; 19:7.

The other word is *shalem*, also used of finishing a building or a work, fulfilling a vow, restoring a debt. Of man it is found: I Kings 8:61; 11:4; 15:3, 14; II Kings 20:3; I Chron. 28:9; 29:19; II Chron. 16:9; 25:2.

The Authorized Version has, in some cases, translated these words by upright or sound. In the Revised Version the word *perfect* has rightly been restored in such passages as Ps. 28:23, 25, "I was also *perfect* with him"; "With the *perfect* man thou wilt show thyself *perfect*." Ps. 19:13, "Then shall I be *perfect*." Ps. 119:1, 80, "Blessed are they that are *perfect* in the way"; "Let my heart be *perfect* in thy statutes."

[2] "If you endeavor to grow in grace, and in all holiness, *trust assuredly that God will en-*

able you. By this manner of walking in the confident persuasion of the privileges of your high state and dignity, *to do everything that is necessary for His glory and your salvation;* and that He graciously accepts of that obedience through Christ which you are enabled to perform according to the measure of your faith, though you fall short of many things as to degrees of holiness and high acts of obedience.

"We are to know that though the law requireth of us the utmost perfection of holiness, yet the gospel maketh an allowance for our weakness. Christ is so meek and lowly in heart that He accepteth of that which our weak faith can attain to by His grace, and doth not exact or expect any more of us for His glory and our salvation until we grow stronger in grace. We are to beware of being too rigorous in exacting righteousness of ourselves and others, beyond the measure of faith and grace. Overdoing commonly proveth undoing."—Marshall, *On Sanctification*, chap. 12.

[3] With the word perfect, and with many other of the words of God that in their divine mystery pass knowledge, pass all understanding, it often is even as with that mysterious Stranger who wrestled with Jacob. He had seized hold upon him but could not prevail, could not overcome him, till he put his thigh out of joint, and made him altogether helpless. It is when our intellect, our creed, our experience all fail us as we seek to master the truth in this word, and we hear the voice, "Let me go!" that we are roused to say, "I will not let thee go except thou bless me." And then, when it has reminded us and made

us confess that our name is Jacob, self-assertion, and given us the promise of a new name and of the hope which that implies, that we shall prevail with God when we are helpless and broken, then, when again we ask its name, we only get the answer, "Wherefore is it that thou asketh after my name?" We want to know and define and name the thing; and it refuses to give a name, for its name is wonderful: it is the hidden wisdom of God in a mystery, which only the Holy Spirit can reveal. And what He reveals, He reveals not always—and just when the blessing is highest, then the least—to the mind, but to the heart, in the inward life; to the faith that accepts the divine, even though it cannot understand. The divine truth in its highest revelation gives no name, but it gives what is better; for we read, "And he blessed him there."

Blessed is the man who sees his God coming to meet him in this mysterious word *perfect;* who no longer seeks to prevail and to master, but yields to it as a power that breaks and masters him, and then says in utter helplessness, "I will not let thee go except thou bless me." Blessed the man who no longer asks to know its name, that he may count it among the things he knows and understands, but is content to let the unknown and unnameable visitant that conquered him bless him there. Yes, blessed the man who ends his wrestlings and begins his rest in the truth of this word *perfect*, in the trembling, adoring exclamation: "I have seen God face to face, and my life is preserved."

[4] Have you ever gone through the 119th Psalm, laying the accent on *Thou, Thee, Thy*

(not omitting the verbs of supplication where the *Thou* is understood)? Use the words as in personal communion with the living God, speaking them into His face, in the assurance that He listens and approves, and is well pleased. Pause at each address to God, till you feel you have said it to Him. So will you learn what the perfect heart is, and what the perfect way is.

And then pray it once again, still speaking as to God, with the accent on the *I, me, mine,* and see what boldness it will give you to say, "With my whole heart *have I* sought thee; consider how *I love* thy testimonies; I love them exceedingly."

[5] The unusual Greek word for perfect is *teleios.* It is derived from *telos,* the end. "This word does not, as is commonly supposed, primarily denote the end or termination with reference to time, but *the goal reached,* the completion or conclusion at which anything arrives, either as *issue* or *ending;* or as result, acme, consummation. It always includes the idea of an inner completion" (Cremer). The adjective is used in a physical or literal sense, of spotless sacrifices, that wherein nothing is deficient, frequently: *full-grown,* of men and beasts; in a moral sense, *perfected, complete, blameless.*

In some of the passages where we have the word perfect in English, the Greek has not the word *teleios* but *katartizein,* from *artios, appropriate, fitting.* The verb means to put a thing in its appropriate position, to put in order; used of equipping, fitting out a ship. Also to bring right again, as of mending nets (Mark 4:21);

of restoring a fallen brother (Gal. 6:1). The idea is making a thing what it should be, so that it is perfect, prepared for the use to which it is destined. *"The perfect and complete setting up* of an object is the main element in the conception. See II Cor. 13:11, of the completion of the Christian character."—Cremer.

Of the texts treated in this little book, this word is used in the following: Luke 6:40; II Cor. 13:9, 11; Heb. 13:21; I Pet. 5:11.

The chief difference between the two words lies in *teleios* having more reference to the inward perfection that comes from growth and development, *katartizein* to that which consists in having defects removed, and what is lacking supplied. Only the former could be used of the Lord Jesus, not the latter. Both are used of us, and the work God and Christ do in us. Both have reference to what God seeks in His children, and works in them.

⁶ I have published in Dutch a devotional exposition of the Epistle to the Hebrews. There some of these thoughts on perfection may be expounded more fully.

⁷ "You are to know, my friends," says William Law, "that every kind of virtue and goodness may be brought into us by two different ways. They may be taught us outwardly by men, by rules, and precepts; and they may be inwardly born in us, as the genuine birth of our own renewed spirit. In the former way, they can at best only change our outward behaviour, and leave our heart in its natural state. Now this way of learning and attaining goodness, though thus

imperfect, *is yet absolutely necessary in the nature of the thing,* and must first have its time and
place and work in us. Yet it is only for a time,
as the law was a schoolmaster to the gospel.
We must first be babes in doctrine, as well as
in strength, before we can be men. But of all this
outward instruction, whether from good men or
from the letter of Scripture, it must be said as
the apostle saith of the law, 'It maketh nothing
perfect,' and yet is highly necessary in order for
perfection. Of these two ways the former is
only in order to the latter, and of no benefit to
us, but as it carries us further than itself, to
be united, in heart and spirit, with the light and
word and Spirit of God."

[8] *Three Friends of God,* by Mrs. Bevan.

[9] "The commands of Jesus together consti-
tute His word. Of this word we cannot choose
out a half or a part to keep. The whole heart
and the whole mind must yield itself completely
to this word, and in simplicity of purpose cling
to it. Then all the truth we know about Jesus
becomes as one word, one thought, that com-
prehends all, one single light in which we behold Jesus. Thus the promise is fulfilled: 'If a
man keep my word, my Father will love him;
and we will come unto him, and dwell with him.'
It is to this John refers: 'He that keepeth his
word, in him verily is the love of God perfected';
that is, it is the truth when such a one says
that God's love has taken complete possession
of his heart, and he lives in it. He experiences
what Jesus spake of the love of the Father resting on Him, and being in Him; his heart is inwardly permeated with it, and filled; so that all

the inclinations, desires, and affections are drawn up into this love, and entirely satisfied with it. The soul now knows and tastes how wonderful the love of God to us sinners is in His Son. It now loves God with all the heart and all the mind. In the inner ground of the heart there is no longer anything halved or divided; there is no more self-will or self-seeking to stand in the way of God's love; the soul gives itself wholly to God with a humbled but wholly satisfied heart. It can now be said: The love of God in Christ has attained its purpose, has got full possession of the heart, sweetly fills all the powers of the soul, and rules over all it does." —Steinhofer on I John.

DAT.

·LI·P170 WILLSON STATIONERS